REMEMBERING
O-SENSEI

O-Sensei cultivated his mind as well as his body. He would start his day with prayer and keiko and close his day with some reading from his large and varied library.

REMEMBERING O-SENSEI

LIVING
AND TRAINING
WITH
MORIHEI UESHIBA,
FOUNDER OF
AIKIDO

Edited by Susan Perry
Foreword by
Moriteru Ueshiba

SHAMBHALA
Boston & London
2002

Shambhala Publications, Inc.
Horticultural Hall
300 Massachusetts Avenue
Boston, Massachusetts 02115
www.shambhala.com

9 8 7 6 5 4 3 2 1

First Edition
Printed in the United States of America

Photos are reprinted with permission from Aikido Archives International,
Michio Hikitsuchi Sensei, and John Stevens.

♾ This edition is printed on acid-free paper that meets the
American National Standards Institute Z39.48 Standard.
Distributed in the United States by Random House, Inc.,
and in Canada by Random House of Canada Ltd

Designed by Ruth Kolbert

Library of Congress Cataloging-in-Publication Data
Remembering O-Sensei: living and training with Morihei Ueshiba,
founder of Aikido/edited by Susan Perry.—1st ed.
p.   cm.
ISBN 1-57062-932-3
1. Ueshiba, Morihei, 1883–1969—Anecdotes.   2. Ueshiba, Morihei,
1883–1969—Friends and associates.   3. Aikido.   I. Perry, Susan.
GV1114.35 .R46 2002
796.815'4—dc21   2002005364

The secret of Aikido
is not in how you move your feet,
it is how you move your mind.
I'm not teaching you martial techniques,
I'm teaching you nonviolence.
MORIHEI UESHIBA

Contents

Foreword

This collection of personal reminiscences about Morihei Ueshiba, the founder of Aikido, has come into being with an outstanding effort by Susan Perry, editor of *Aikido Today Magazine*.

From the beginning of her project, I have had a keen interest in the book and have eagerly awaited its publication. I hope that a great number of people will get to know Aikido through this book, and also that Aikido practitioners will be inspired to study the art more thoroughly. I am sure that this book will help people to properly and deeply understand the spirit of

Aikido taught by the Founder. It is my sincere hope that this book will provide a positive influence on Aikido practitioners throughout the world.

MORITERU UESHIBA
Aikido Doshu
Tokyo, January 2002

Acknowledgments

I was very pleased when Shambhala Publications approached me about doing a collection of stories about O-Sensei. I am proud to have been able to present this volume of stories and thankful that I have been able to interview so many inspiring teachers over the past fifteen years.

I am indebted to my editor, Beth Frankl, for bringing this project to me and for her cheerful encouragement along the way. Many people have contributed to this project in innumerable ways: they encouraged me, helped with translation or typing, helped with my travels to Japan and my interviews there, helped in securing photos of O-Sensei, and helped me carry on my work at *Aikido Today Magazine* while I was busy working on this project. These people are: James Bradford, Tim Detmer, David Durdines, Nikki Gabany, Laurin Herr, Kevin Karr, Nia Kaye, Philip Ma, Brent Magnusson, Cecelia Munoz, Sumi Nakono, Neil Segal, and John Schleis.

I greatly appreciate the support and help extended to me by the present Doshu, Moriteru Ueshiba, and his staff at Aikikai Hombu Dojo. Also, I am very grateful to all the people whose interviews I included in this book, and for the help from the following sensei: Kazuaki Tanahashi, Mary Heiny, Motomichi Anno, John Stevens, and Michio Hikitsuchi.

Finally, I thank my husband, Ronald G. Rubin, whose deep understanding and loving respect for the mystery of life encourage, inspire, and sustain me throughout our journey together.

Introduction

Morihei Ueshiba (1883–1969), to whom Aikido practitioners refer as "O-Sensei," was one of the world's most celebrated martial artists. His gift was to marry effective martial technique with a deep spirituality. A master of many martial arts, he brought out of budo (the martial path) a deep philosophical element. His influence on philosophical thinkers as well as martial artists has been profound.

O-Sensei traveled widely in Japan, perfecting his art by talking with other visionaries and by successfully engaging in physical challenges. His reputation as a man of budo grew.

Many students were drawn to him. Many became his *uchi*

deshi (live-in students). The uchi deshi system was a common Japanese way of learning—similar to, but not exactly the same as, Western apprenticeship. The students lived on the same premises as their teacher and became involved in many aspects of their teacher's daily life.

Aikido is an art of spiritual transmission. Although O-Sensei was a religious man, as some of the stories in this book will reveal, I do not mean to suggest that what O-Sensei transmitted to his students was a religion, but that he was moved to help people discover deep reverence for life and "the spirit of loving protection for all creation."

O-Sensei's uchi deshi were expected to tend to his needs twenty-four hours a day. Whether he needed to practice a technique in the middle of the night, to travel to another city to teach, to have someone massage his sore muscles, to welcome a visitor, or to farm, uchi deshi were expected to be ready to help him. In this way, they could see how the principles of Aikido extended into all facets of life. For his students, O-Sensei was a model of Aikido.

Philosophical treatises and abstract philosophy seldom inspire people to act—but human examples of honorable living can instill hope and inspire action. People take as their aims what seems possible and good. If someone lives a virtuous life, others can see that such a life is possible. Mother Teresa and Gandhi are examples of humble and unselfish living, and stories of Jesus, Buddha, and Mohammed have helped people throughout the ages to frame their lives so that they can understand how to make them better. In this way, O-Sensei, too, inspires many people.

Many of O-Sensei's students took up the challenge to spread Aikido philosophy. In so doing, they have introduced it to an increasingly international audience. O-Sensei's students are now the leaders of Aikido around the world. But, they are growing older. Their recollections of O-Sensei have been handed down to their students, serving to inspire them. In what has become an oral history, our glimpse of O-Sensei's vision of Aikido comes from the recollections of those who were around him.

O-Sensei's lessons were not always the same for every student. Instead, he matched his lessons to what he perceived as a student's interests and abilities. Accordingly, his live-in students as well as students who trained more briefly under his authority came away with different perspectives of the art and different stories about their teacher.

In this book I have brought many of these stories together. Through them, readers will see how O-Sensei interacted with the world, how he behaved off the mat when he was with friends and family, how he was as a teacher, and as a public spokesman, how he handled responsibility, what angered him, and what he thought was important. As you read through these many stories, a portrait of O-Sensei will come together that provides a more realistic understanding of his vision and of his art.

Aikido is a transformative art. Seeing Aikido's martial techniques through the broader perspective of O-Sensei's life reveals the art's principles and how they apply to everyday life. The application of these principles is what O-Sensei demonstrated for his live-in students.

One of the things that caught their attention is that O-Sensei was both a compassionate and a kind teacher as well as a powerful and a ferocious martial artist. It is this combination of contradictory qualities that makes O-Sensei a fascinating and inspiring person.

Another thing that they realized is that to learn the deeper lessons of Aikido is to transform one's self into a person with a larger and more powerful capacity for living well. O-Sensei presented his students with the model of the person who lived with courage, sensitivity, and virtue. If this model is available to us, it is through the sort of stories I have collected here.

This book is divided into four chapters. "First Meetings" highlights students' experiences with O-Sensei the first time they met him. Because O-Sensei didn't separate physical training from spiritual training, the chapter, "Training," focuses primarily on lessons students received while they were on the mat. "Daily Living" reveals O-Sensei's habits, likes and dislikes, and approach to everyday life. The final chapter, "Art of Peace," gives more of a sense of O-Sensei's spiritual vision.

I hope you enjoy reading these stories as much as I have enjoyed collecting them, and I hope that those who practice Aikido will allow the stories to influence their training. I invite those who have O-Sensei stories that are not included in this collection to send them to me. I would be happy to put another collection together.

Susan Perry
Claremont, California
December 2001

REMEMBERING
O-SENSEI

O-Sensei poses displaying the Medal of Honor
he received from the Japanese Government.

1

FIRST
MEETINGS

TIRED FROM TRAVELING AND LOOKING FORWARD TO MORE DIFFICULT WORK ahead, the young man looked for a seat on the crowded train. Settling next to a stocky old man, he sat back against the swaying side of the car. "Don't I know you?" asked the old man next to him. Sighing, the young man looked over into the wrinkling face beside him. "I don't think so." "Yes, I'm sure I know you," said the old man. "What is your name?" The young man sat up and faced his new companion more directly. Looking fiercely at the old man, he announced proudly. "I am Kenshiro Abbe, Judo champion of all Japan." The old man smiled. "Ah, yes. I knew I had seen you before." "Please, could you be quiet now," asked Abbe, settling back in his seat. "I have a competition I am going to and I need to get some rest." "Of course," said the old man. As the train ground along the winding track, however, the old man didn't stop talking. He continued to drone on incessantly, till finally Abbe sat up and again faced him. "Be quiet, old man," he said. "I need to sleep." "If I am just an old man and you are such a great Judo champion, then perhaps you can break my finger. I will be quiet if you can break my little finger," said the old man. Thinking that he may finally be rid of the old man, the young man scrutinized the single digit that was held out to him. Tired and a little angry, he grabbed the finger and twisted it to break it. What followed, however, wasn't the dry small snapping sound he'd expected. Instead he was airborne—slammed down onto the floor of the train, with all of the air escaped from his lungs. Worse still, he was immobilized. After a moment, the old man let him up. "Who are you?" asked Abbe in wonderment. "I am Morihei Ueshiba, founder of Aikido," said the old man. Abbe, still on the floor of the car, bowed to the old man and asked if he could come to his dojo (place of training) to train. He was accepted as a student and would stay with Ueshiba for ten years.

KENSHIRO ABBE

Admiral Isamu Takeshita was a teacher of Jujitsu who was very interested in martial arts. In O-Sensei's movements, Admiral Takeshita saw the motion of battleships. So he was very impressed with O-Sensei. Admiral Takeshita told the founder of Judo, Kano Sensei, about O-Sensei.

Having asked O-Sensei to teach at the naval academy, Admiral Takeshita invited Kano Sensei to observe class. When Kano Sensei saw O-Sensei, he said, "This is very good. Will you please teach my students?"

MINORU MOCHIZUKI

When I first saw O-Sensei, I immediately felt that O-Sensei was not an ordinary person. Even though he was short and had a beard, he had a noble manner about him. In particular, his face was very dignified and solemn, and he appeared to be someone who possessed a very high level of spirituality.

GUJI YUKITAKA YAMAMOTO

My friend said to me one day, "An incredibly strong old guy has shown up in Shingu. Let's go together to take a look." The dojo was new; O-Sensei had come for the first time. O-Sensei was there with some of his *deshi* (students) he had brought, and they were training. One of the deshi was a woman. As I was watching the practice and staring at this woman, O-Sensei came up and said, "Get a *keikogi* (training uniform) on and start practicing."

I knew nothing about Aikido. I had no experience of it. But O-Sensei told me to train with the woman. I thought that I could not lose to some young woman; I was quite strong when I was young. So, I got on a keikogi and got on the mat to work out with that woman. But, to my surprise, no matter what I did, I was trounced and bounced around. She did *shihonage* on me over and over. O-Sensei never taught *ukemi* (the movements of the partner, *uke*, including attacking and sometimes falling), he just said that you learn it by doing it. Then I asked O-Sensei if I could be his student. He said I needed to have two sponsors. So, I got two sponsors and entered the dojo and began Aikido.

YUUICHI NAKAGUCHI

When I first met O-Sensei, I was fascinated by the atmosphere that surrounded him. He was completely different from what I imagined a martial artist to be. O-Sensei seemed to have a divine sense of purpose. He communicated the idea that anyone could improve his or her inner self through continued practice of Aikido.

MAMORU SUGANUMA

The Ueshibas have ordered keikogi from me for many years. Once when I was delivering the keikogi I had made for the Ueshibas, I walked into the old dojo during practice. People were on the mat practicing and suddenly O-Sensei came into the room. Now, I had heard of O-Sensei but had never met him and didn't know anything about him. And when he came into the room, suddenly everybody at the same time sat down and bowed and there was this great show of reverence toward him. I was tremendously impressed by how the posture of the students reflected their attitude of respect and reverence toward O-Sensei, and I thought he must be a very splendid teacher. I was struck by this perception. When O-Sensei taught, he had a strict demeanor, but when he was off the mat, he was very kind and gentle.

AYAKO ISHIWATA

When I first saw O-Sensei, he was sitting in the living room next to a charcoal brazier. O-Sensei was wearing a kimono, and he looked like a mountain hermit, not an ordinary human being. I was very drawn to him.

O-Sensei asked about the family who introduced me and also talked of stories of olden times (legends and so forth). So I entered the dojo that day. I wasn't at that time able to talk to O-Sensei about anything deep.

SADATERU ARIKAWA

The very moment I met O-Sensei I thought he was a very great person. O-Sensei's eyes were incredibly sharp. At the same time, in back of this sharp gaze was the light of an indescribable kindness and tenderness. My first impression was that the light that shone from O-Sensei's eyes was fearsome and kind at the same time.

SEISEKI ABE

In 1947, two years after the end of WWII, I was in junior high school. It was at this time that my mother, my two younger brothers, and I went to Iwama to live in a thatched-roofed, one-room hut attached to O-Sensei's Iwama dojo.

O-Sensei offered a nightly class for five or six of us village kids. Every night he would give us *keiko* (training). At first when I looked into the dojo, I saw people falling down like cats and doing other strange things. At times, they seemed to be doing something archaic, like an ancient prayer. I didn't want to join them. But O-Sensei invited me in, and I thought I should try. I went along and, in time, got used to the rolling and movement. I was attracted to the spiritual atmosphere.

At the beginning, it was horrible, but I got used to it. Of course, in our practice we did very simple things. We would do the same things over and over, every day. I think that every season we started out with seated *kokyu waza* and ended with kokyu waza.

Japan had been disarmed after its surrender, and no martial arts were allowed. People were embarrassed about military things; anything that had to do with warriors or defense was unpopular. Few people were practicing martial arts. It is possible that, at that time, this small group of young boys and O-Sensei were the only existing Aikido class in Japan—perhaps even in the world.

O-Sensei's dojo was quite small, and it had a wooden floor. There was an altar. Inside the dojo building, there also was a waiting room with tatami—maybe eight mats.

O-Sensei's house was about 500 feet away. The Aiki Jinja (shrine) was between the house and the dojo. The electrical supply was very low at the time, and the power often went off. We would have lights for fifteen minutes or so, and then it would get dark again. We would sit and wait in the waiting room without saying anything. What was remarkable was that O-Sensei's eyes would glare even in the darkness, like cats' eyes.

KAZUAKI TANAHASHI

One day a friend came and said that a strange teacher had come to Iwama. We made a date to go together to visit this teacher, but my friend got scared and didn't show up. I came to see a morning class. Uchi deshi were there. O-Sensei owned a lot of land in Iwama, and so he built a house, a shrine, and a dojo. His house was small.

At the time I went to sign up, I first went over to O-Sensei's house. A student was sitting outside. I said, "I've come to join the dojo." He told me that O-Sensei was in the dojo and class was in progress. I went over to the dojo. I was just eighteen at the time. I was wearing a shirt and pants and asked if I could train. O-Sensei looked at me and said that if I was just going to train for a little bit and leave, it would be a bother for him and would serve no purpose for him. But if I thought I could continue to practice, I could start. So, I entered the dojo and started. O-Sensei told me that I should practice with the view of being of service to others and the world.

MORIHIRO SAITO

In the beginning of the 1950s, a Karate teacher told me about a thrilling experience. He said, "I have met a man who's like a phantom. I tried to punch him, but I couldn't reach him at all." The man was O-Sensei.

SHOJI NISHIO

The second day I was at Hombu Dojo, O-Sensei came out and put on an unbelievable demonstration for thirty minutes. I was mesmerized by O-Sensei's movement.

HENRY KONO

O-Sensei's student, Hikitsuchi, brought him to the Tsubaki shrine for the first time in 1959. When O-Sensei got here, he immediately went into the waterfall to do waterfall *misogi* (purification practice). My father and I went into the water also. O-Sensei came out of the waterfall and did *bo* (a long wooden staff) practice with chanting for about an hour. I didn't understand what it was at that time. We then went to my home, and we all had tea together. After that, every year he came with his student Hikitsuchi.

GUJI YUKITAKA YAMAMOTO

When O-Sensei visited Hawaii, the hosting teachers had no trouble translating the opening of his talks, because he would take time in greeting his audience and thanking them for coming. But after that, he would talk about fire and water, and we translators were lost.

TAKASHI NONAKA

When I first arrived at Hombu Dojo from Hawaii, I offered my letter of recommendation to a man in the front office. The office clerk said, "Just a minute," and disappeared. From where I stood, I could see inside the dojo. Right next to the office was a little room and that room was for O-Sensei and his son, Kisshomaru Doshu; it was their office or sitting room. They were both sitting there having tea that day. The office clerk returned and took me in to meet O-Sensei and Kisshomaru Doshu.

I had read one or two books on Aikido. I had read that O-Sensei was the master, and I had seen some pictures of him. Upon entering, I was struck by how O-Sensei's eyes twinkled. I would swear he had blue eyes, but I knew that Japanese didn't have blue eyes, so they couldn't have been blue. But they were so bright and they were so twinkly that it just struck me. Somehow being in his presence, I realized I was meeting a remarkable man! I stammered in my schoolboy Japanese. They sat and made light conversation. O-Sensei didn't know what to do with me, but he was polite and gave me tea. Finally Kisshomaru Doshu said,

"Well three o'clock class is starting." I had my keikogi and followed Kisshomaru Doshu out so that I could change for class.

ROBERT FRAGER

In any love affair, there are many first meetings. There's the literal one, the first time you met, and then there's the first time you *saw*. There's the first time you felt, and then there's the first time those came together. So there's a series of "firsts."

The first time I really saw O-Sensei was the first time that he asked me to attack him. I'd watched these other people attack him, and it seemed interesting, like here's this little old man and these guys would attack him, and they would fall down. I was a little skeptical. But then he asked *me* to attack him. I didn't know what that meant. Talk about culture shock! In my culture, you're not supposed to hit old people on the head. I knew he wanted me to hit him on the head as hard as I could. I knew that. And I was terrified.

I was terrified for several reasons. One, because I was going in the face of a cultural law that you don't hit old people on the head. Two, there are all these black belts sitting around. If I hit him on the head, I'm going to get killed. If I kill him, they're going to kill me.

Then I thought, if I kill him and they kill me, then I won't have to study Aikido; I'll be dead. Or if I don't hit him on the head, then I won't have to study, because we will have entered into an agreement of deception: "OK, I'll go here, you go here; I agree not to hit you, and I'll fall down when you yell at me, when you throw me." But I wasn't interested in participating in anything theatrical.

The first time I couldn't really bring myself to hit him. So, when I came, I was asking a question. I don't know what he did,

9

O-Sensei took pleasure in all that he did but even while relaxing, he never let his guard down.

he grabbed me, he put me on the ground. I don't know what he said, but what he meant was "is that the best you can do, is that the most concentration you can give me." It really pissed me off. I thought, "well, I don't care how old you are, I'm going to try for real." So the next time I stood up, I really tried to hit his head. The next thing I know, I'm looking up. He's looking down and he's asking, "Are you all right?" There was no interval. I remember the determination and I remember focusing, triangulating on the spot on his head. The next minute, I'm looking up. There's been no passage of time—just here, and then there.

I realized that something very important had happened for me. Maybe this was a trick. Maybe this was a form of participatory hypnosis, a self-induced trance or something like that. But if it was, then I wanted to learn how to do that. It was definitely not theatrical. It did not require my conscious participation. And that really impressed me very much. I realized that this was something different.

TERRY DOBSON

I went to Japan to study with O-Sensei; I had heard that he was a great martial artist and, upon seeing him in action, I was impressed. But like most Americans, I needed convincing. One day O-Sensei looked at me and told me to grab his arm. I was in very good shape then and thought that this was my chance to check O-Sensei out. I reached for his arm. After I grabbed for his arm, the next thing I knew I was in a different realm—a different dimension—for what felt like a very long time. Then, as I bounced out of that dimension and back into the space of the dojo, O-Sensei appeared to me on my right side, I felt a tingle on my forehead just before I went down hard onto the mat. Everybody laughed because my mouth was open in awe. It was an entirely new experience for me. My body had crossed a line that very few people ever cross, and my crossing that line had not had anything to do with how long I had been training in Aikido.

ROBERT NADEAU

It was a special Sunday morning practice on a lovely spring day. The birds were singing and the windows were open. As was customary, the first person to see O-Sensei clapped, and the students all scurried to the side of the dojo and sat in *seiza* (traditional Japanese sitting position). O-Sensei may have just been passing through the dojo on his way from his living quarters to his office, but, as he very often did, he stopped for a moment to teach.

O-Sensei asked a student for a *shomenuchi* attack with a *bokken* (wooden sword). As the attack came, O-Sensei drew his little fan from his belt and let out the most incredible *kiai* (shout). Hearing it really was a shattering experience. The kiai had a startling effect on me—I trembled and couldn't control myself. I couldn't believe what was happening to me!

After a few minutes, O-Sensei went on his way and the class ended. Immediately after class, the two or three foreigners who were there all rushed to each other. We had all experienced the same thing.

KEN COTTIER

I first saw O-Sensei when he gave an incredible demonstration. All the top teachers came for this demonstration. It was given before the emperor of Manchuria.

SHINGENOBU OKUMURA

The first Aikido class I saw was taught by O-Sensei. When O-Sensei came into the room, there was a twinkling feeling; everybody stopped training and sat down, and O-Sensei began to demonstrate. He did things like becoming immovable or throwing people without touching them, things that defied physics.

As I watched O-Sensei's unbelievable demonstrations, I had a very bizarre experience. I felt as though my brain blew out of my head and hovered over me like a cloud of sand. I felt split in two. One part of me somehow understood what was going on and knew that a very profound truth was being demonstrated. The other part of me said, "He's an old man, and Japanese treat old people with respect. Maybe his partners are just falling down for him." I just felt that this man had some profound knowledge of how things worked in the universe— knowledge that lay completely outside my education and experience. But, at the same time, I was suspicious: At that point in my life, everything had to be reasonable and logical, or I would have nothing to do with it.

At the end of the demonstration, O-Sensei walked off the mat and paused. When he was opposite me at the door that led into his house, he turned, and I thought that he looked at me. I heard later that he was very nearsighted; maybe he was just gazing into the distance. But what I experienced was that he looked at me. I had a very clear impression of his eyes, and I felt a light come from them into my abdomen. I felt a flower-opening sensation.

People say that, when you're about to die, your whole life flashes before your eyes. I had an experience of that sort, and everything made sense to me. It seemed to me that everything that had happened to me had inevitably led to this exact moment, and I felt that Aikido was my path.

MARY HEINY

13

One of O-Sensei's amazing demonstrations.

2

TRAINING

I CAME TO AIKIDO HAVING STUDIED JUDO
AND KARATE IN THE MARINE CORPS, SO
I thought of martial arts in terms of strength and speed. Initially I had a great deal of cynicism about what I saw O-Sensei doing.

But then I would attack O-Sensei at one place, and, all of a sudden, I would find O-Sensei in another place. I couldn't believe what I felt and saw in O-Sensei's Aikido dojo. But, I had never challenged O-Sensei directly.

O-Sensei did this fantastic demonstration where he would invite his students to push against the side of a bokken he was holding out before him. It seemed unreal. I became increasingly skeptical of this demonstration, because O-Sensei would always call for students other than me to push against the bokken. I began thinking that they were all part of a grand hoax O-Sensei was putting over on his audience.

One day I was part of a demonstration. This time when O-Sensei began this demonstration with the bokken, I ran up with the other students. Three students were already pushing on the bokken O-Sensei was holding. When I made contact with that bokken, I was certain it would move or give just a little bit. But even though I slammed into the bokken; there was no give, nothing budged, not even a bit. There was less movement than in a wall. It was like hitting solid steel. How O-Sensei managed that I'll never know. I remember that feeling to this day—one of the biggest surprises in my life. What I do know is that all my experience in the world as a human being can't help me explain that experience.

TERRY DOBSON

When O-Sensei threw students who didn't often take ukemi for him, they would get up with a stupefied expression on their face as if they were saying to themselves "what happened?" I never saw him move, I never felt him move. It felt like he just stood there and I moved. I was about twenty-five and a brand new *shodan* (black belt). But nevertheless I have never before or since experienced anything like it. He just stood there and I fell. O-Sensei would then say things like, "When you attack me you are trying to attack the whole universe."

ROBERT FRAGER

Students all felt in their own bodies that O-Sensei had an amazingly strong *kokyu* (breath) power. They could never reach O-Sensei however much they attacked him, so they felt there was something terrific inside him, something that was not visible.

YUUICHI NAKAGUCHI

O-Sensei's posture was most impressive. He never slumped or broke his posture. It wasn't just his form; he always had absolutely perfect posture. It was very surprising. One never saw O-Sensei lean over at the dojo or in front of someone, put his hand down, and say "I'm pooped." Either O-Sensei had no opening or he never showed any opening. Even the person with whom he was most relaxed said that O-Sensei never let his guard down or lessened his awareness.

Even when students were just sitting around talking with O-Sensei, they could not sense any openings. No matter how fast or hard students attacked, they could never get him. Doubtless this was the bewitching appeal of O-Sensei, which has kept drawing students to Aikido even today.

MOTOMICHI ANNO

O-Sensei was very strong for his size. One time O-Sensei performed with an uchi deshi, using solid wood swords. But the student hit O-Sensei on the head, which made a loud noise. I thought O-Sensei was injured badly, but he wasn't hurt at all.

SEISEKI ABE

O-Sensei's ending positions were great and natural, and his movement showed really exquisite rhythm. Like music, sometimes he was very slow, so subtle he almost seemed not to move at all, and then sometimes he was so fast and changed so quickly you could not see it. He moved from slow motion to very powerful motion, like lightning.

KAZUAKI TANAHASHI

Once O-Sensei was in the Osaka area and visited all the universities. At a particular demonstration, O-Sensei said, "Is there anyone among you who has doubts about me and wants to attack this old man? If so, come and attack." One person in the audience yelled out "I will!" Many in the audience thought O-Sensei's demonstrations were fake. They could not understand how an old man with slumped shoulders who looked like he could barely stand could defeat strong young men. This one doubter stood to attack O-Sensei. He rushed up to grab O-Sensei's neck and wrist, but suddenly he felt something that he later described as a tremendous ball of fire fly at him. Then he flew through the air. It was frightening. O-Sensei must have projected his *ki* (universal energy or life force). It is something you can't see. This inner ki strength is what was so amazing about O-Sensei. Others can imitate his form, but they don't have this inner quality. There is some quality to Aikido that can't be seen. It is not just form. That is why Aikido is fearsome.

YUUICHI NAKAGUCHI

I'm big, and O-Sensei was little. We were a perfect theatrical match. Sometimes in demonstration, he would call me up to grab his shoulder, and he'd say, "Why do you grab my beard? I'm an old man." The first time he said it, I was terribly embarrassed, because it was in front of a whole bunch of people. Everyone laughed. He said, "I'm just an old man, I don't have many hairs in my beard. If you grab them and pull them out, I'll look terrible." Everybody laughed. It was a good joke.

TERRY DOBSON

One time O-Sensei sat knee to knee in seiza with me. O-Sensei said, "Put your hands out." He put one hand over mine, and he said, "push." To me, O-Sensei's hand felt as light as a feather. Even when I pushed as hard as I could, O-Sensei's hand did not change; I didn't move either! Nothing moved. I had this moment of absolutely experiencing something that was clearly phenomenal, I couldn't move, and the amazing thing was that his hand felt like a feather, like nothing. So, I realized whatever the hell was going on, *he* was doing it. And I thought, when I attack him at full speed, and I can't feel anything but that feather feeling and he's still stopping me cold—whatever he's doing, I don't know what it is!

ROBERT FRAGER

O-Sensei's body was not hard; it was soft. And yet those who grabbed him always spoke of their power draining away. It was as though his body negated or absorbed your power.

MOTOICHI YANASE

Sometimes when O-Sensei touched me, I felt my power suddenly increase; then again, sometimes when O-Sensei touched me, I felt my strength drain away. Even if I came close to O-Sensei, it seemed my strength was absorbed. I also felt a

tremendous pressure sometimes. It was the strength of the
kami (divine energy). O-Sensei was very strong, and his arms
were huge. It was terrifying. I thought I would be broken.

MICHIO HIKITSUCHI

Every day O-Sensei would do something extraordinary. I
couldn't really believe my eyes. It was like a miracle every day.
We would push him, and he wouldn't move. He would throw
people without effort. Or he would pin a person using just one
finger. He would talk to us in a very relaxed way, while the person he was pinning would struggle to get up. That was something he really liked to do. I think it may have been the way he
was exerting his ki.

Whatever O-Sensei said was spiritual—and impossible to
comprehend. Also, O-Sensei would often say that Aikido is a
path of no resistance and, although it seemed contradictory,
that it is a path of challenging the spirit. He said that Aikido
embodies the circle, triangle, and square.

KAZUAKI TANAHASHI

O-Sensei enjoyed himself. He was natural. Whatever he had to
say for that day, he said. He might chuckle and smile or he
might growl and yell, but he enjoyed every minute. Sometimes
he would come over, put his finger over a student, and hold
that student down so that the student couldn't move. One time
O-Sensei held me without any direct physical contact—a no-
touch hold. There was strength beyond the physical. Those
who have been around O-Sensei know that when you come up
against a spirit like his, you are coming up against something

that you have to back away from when it's projected toward you. It's very beautiful and supremely powerful.

VIRGINIA MAYHEW

Once we went to a very stuffy men's club in Osaka. A small group of people were sitting around in what looked like a big, very formal living room, drinking tea or coffee. O-Sensei knew many of them; they were retired military people and business leaders.

O-Sensei was dressed normally, but he had me change into my keikogi and *hakama* (divided skirt, part of the Aikido training uniform) and started throwing me. The trouble was that there was no place to land. The room was filled with coffee tables, glass trophy cases, and people in overstuffed chairs, balancing teacups on their laps. O-Sensei threw me between one chair and another, leaving it to me to turn in midair and to avoid blasting an industrialist with my feet. I sailed one way and the other, while O-Sensei was talking about mythology!

TERRY DOBSON

O-Sensei would often thunder, "These techniques are only for health! What Aikido is about is spiritual."

ROBERT FRAGER

O-Sensei wore a white belt all his life and he had no ranking in Aikido; he was completely above all that.

SHINGENOBU OKUMURA

O-Sensei displays his ability to center despite students' attempts to move him.

O-Sensei could do things that no one else could do. One time I approached him about this. Noting my observation, I asked him what he was doing differently. He told me that I would find the secret in yin and yang.

HENRY KONO

When O-Sensei did Aikido, his eyes became very shiny and sharp. Also, if he was in a formal situation and he saw some people behaving rudely, he would have sharp, piercing eyes. O-Sensei showed his fierce or sharp gaze more before the war than after the war."

SADATERU ARIKAWA

O-Sensei had an interesting color of gray eyes, which he could use to move people. He would seemingly call up an uke by making some very small gesture and directing those eyes, and the uke would almost be brought up by his very look.

MASAKI TANI

Sometimes O-Sensei would look people in the eye. If O-Sensei glared directly at someone, they just wilted. Some people didn't want to be called out by O-Sensei and would try to avoid his view, but others would sit in front, hoping to be called out. Some people would try to hide, only to be called anyway.

SADATERU ARIKAWA

It is difficult to describe O-Sensei for several reasons. One is because he was very hard to look at. He controlled you. Not consciously, but when he was in the room, you knew he was there, and you knew where he was in the room all the time. You could look at him, you could talk to him, but he'd look straight at you. It might be wonderful; I might look at him and see a nice grandfather one day. Or it could be awful; I'd look at him, and he'd be a dragon with the fire of hell coming out of his eyes. I wouldn't want to look. I never figured out if what you saw depended on O-Sensei's mood or what shape you were in.

TERRY DOBSON

When O-Sensei was doing a demonstration, there would come a point where his eyes became almost purple and he would seem to enter another world. At that point, it would just become a magnificent demonstration. I could see his eyes change.

SHINGENOBU OKUMURA

O-Sensei moved around slowly when he was older, but when he stepped on the mat, he came alive. He taught *ikkyo* and *iriminage* and did not teach more complicated techniques like *kotegaeshi* or shihonage.

MASAKI TANI

As O-Sensei approached his mid-eighties, illness and time began to take their toll. He grew thin and his step was slowed. He needed help climbing stairs, and with each movement of his body, he experienced severe pain. Yet throughout his illness, he still taught Aikido. The moment he stepped onto the mat, he was transformed from an aging man enduring his last suffering into a man who could not be defeated by another man, nor by death itself. His presence was commanding. His eyes sparkled and his body vibrated with power. He effortlessly threw his uchi deshi, all of whom were young, strong, experienced from daily training, and at the peak of physical condition. Showing no sign of pain or discomfort, he laughed at our determined attempts to attack or hold him. In demonstration he would extend his wooden sword in front of him and encourage five of us at a time to push on it from the side with all our might. We could not move him or the bokken an inch. It would have been easier to move a wall.

MITSUGI SAOTOME

I was very young when I studied with O-Sensei; there were about fifty years between us, and our interests were very different. As a young man, I was not interested in O-Sensei's philosophy or in Shinto. Like other young men, I was only interested in becoming physically strong by learning the mysteries of power that I believed Aikido held. I wanted to beat the strong people, the practitioners of Kendo, Judo, and so on.

As an older man myself, I now can understand why O-Sensei was interested in philosophy and Shinto. O-Sensei was trying to teach us how, through Aikido, we could rid ourselves of illusion and begin to discover reality.

NOBUYOSHI TAMURA

Once, when a woman correspondent from France came to the dojo, O-Sensei was so sick he couldn't even stand up. The woman pleaded with him to give a demonstration, saying that she was never coming back to Japan again. So, O-Sensei consented. Students had to carry him onto the mat on a litter. They stood him up, and he told his ukes to attack. Suddenly, he was a different man. He put on a twenty-minute demonstration, almost nonstop. He just said, "Keep coming!" It was awesome. But, when it was over, he couldn't stand up any more. Students had to put him back on the litter and carry him off the mat.

Physically, he was an eighty-six-year-old man. For a man of this age to put on a twenty-minute demonstration nonstop—that alone should have shown people that he was doing something fantastic! Even when O-Sensei was old and sick, when he got on the mat he was a different man.

HENRY KONO

When O-Sensei came here, I shared everyday life with him in my own house for eight to ten days on each visit. O-Sensei got up at six in the winter and at five in the summer while he was staying here. O-Sensei would practice various esoteric practices every morning when he arose. Among his practices was the opening recitation of a long *norito* (prayer) called *Oharai Norito* (prayer of great purification). O-Sensei would get up and do misogi and then at the beginning of practice would recite the Oharai Norito. We would sit behind him and follow his lead. I would study and try to imitate his breathing, his phrasing, how he projected his voice. It became my kokyu study. After class I would ask him about all the kami names that were in the prayer and he would give a clear explanation. This is the routine that would happen at the dojo when O-Sensei stayed here. O-Sensei emphasized that the purpose of Aikido training is not technical but spiritual. O-Sensei said to people that they should connect their life's work or their life's purpose to their Aikido.

SEISEKI ABE

There was no pattern to O-Sensei's on-the-mat-teaching. It was divine working. Always starting with ikkyo *suwariwaza* he would then move according to his ki of the moment.

MICHIO HIKITSUCHI

O-Sensei insisted that students focus on the basics (*kihon*). For him the basics were posture, breathing, and attitude. He believed that a human being has a body and a spirit and that body and spirit should work together.

NOBUYOSHI TAMURA

When I began Aikido, only adults twenty-five and older could train. To be a student of O-Sensei's, you were required to have five sponsors. Not everyone could study Aikido.

MICHIO HIKITSUCHI

At that time there was no tuition. To give money to O-Sensei, the student put money in an envelope and wrote *"tamagushi"* (offering) on it and put it on the shrine. Some would bring rice or vegetables, something in exchange for lessons. Nowadays there is not only tuition but there is also tax on the tuition! In the old days, people had little money.

SHINGENOBU OKUMURA

If O-Sensei heard that someone had gotten hurt, he would lecture students for forty minutes. He said that nobody needed to get hurt.

Also, O-Sensei hated push-ups because they use muscle, but guys used to do them. If O-Sensei saw them doing push-ups, he'd make them all sit down and give them another lecture.

HENRY KONO

Once an Aikido student had died while training in Osaka. This was rarely heard of, but apparently the student was taking a high fall and landed on his neck. It was not someone O-Sensei knew or had ever seen. The dojo in which this student died was on the other side of Japan, hundreds of miles away. But O-Sensei was very, very upset. Very upset. He felt responsible. O-Sensei may not have even trained the guy that was teaching that day. But O-Sensei felt responsible for everything that happened on every Aikido mat. It is a far bigger way of being in the world than most of us can imagine.

ROBERT FRAGER

On the mat, O-Sensei really hated it when students struggled with each other, pushed each other, or tried to use force. These things were completely against his Aikido. When he was away, some youngsters would have fun competing in wrestling with one another. But that was completely opposite from what O-Sensei was teaching.

At the Iwama dojo, very simple movements were a regular part of the practice. But because the dojo was small, only one

Through O-Sensei's strict gaze one could detect an indescribable kindness and tenderness.

pair could work at one time. O-Sensei was strict. He would sometimes smile, but he wouldn't tell jokes. He didn't do or say anything wasteful. He was always focused on the spiritual life, and Aikido was a part of that life.

KAZUAKI TANAHASHI

When there was a request for Aikido in foreign countries, senior Aikido students would be sent to help spread understanding of the art. O-Sensei always advised them to become people of the country in which they lived—to assimilate.

MITSUGI SAOTOME

One day O-Sensei saw some students practicing old pre-WWII forms. He scolded and lectured them, saying, "Why do you think I have spent so much time perfecting the art?"

YOSHIMITSU YAMADA

O-Sensei liked the flower and the pine tree. The uchi deshi would hit the pine tree for bokken practice, and O-Sensei would hear this and get pissed off. He would come out and say, "You're killing the tree!"

In an old movie there is some footage showing O-Sensei practicing *jo* (a wooden staff used in Aikido training) with a tree, but he tied protective armor around the tree.

MITSUGI SAOTOME

When students became proficient in their Aikido study, they would teach classes. Some developed university Aikido clubs.

For groups like this, instructors would often hold *gasshukus*; a special three or four day event where students would eat, sleep, and train together. So one time a teacher named Tomita was holding such a gasshuku at the Iwama dojo.

The tradition is if you are at another teacher's dojo, even though you are scheduled to teach a class, you go to that teacher and you ask permission to teach the class. This is expected even when the teacher is so sick that he clearly cannot get out of bed. If you were to teach a class when O-Sensei was around, especially if you were at the Iwama dojo, you'd have two good reasons to ask O-Sensei's permission: the Iwama dojo was not only a dojo that O-Sensei built, but he was the founder of Aikido. So, if O-Sensei was present, you would never just teach Aikido without checking with him first. If he wanted to teach it, it was his class.

Tomita had asked O-Sensei if he wanted to teach the morning class of the gasshuku. Although O-Sensei did not teach that class, the students trained for a couple hours in the morning, had lunch, and cleaned up around the dojo. When it was time for the afternoon class, O-Sensei was napping. Tomita decided he was not going to bother O-Sensei by waking him to ask his permission to teach. After all, the class was for a bunch of college kids and O-Sensei was not in Iwama to teach college kids. So, poor Tomita went ahead and started class.

After only a couple of throws, O-Sensei was up and striding into the dojo with fire in his eyes. I was in between O-Sensei and Tomita; the energy was so intense I really wanted to flip the tatami mats up and go under the dojo. It was like being in the path of a typhoon. O-Sensei was angry, and I was in his path to Tomita. O-Sensei went on and on about the importance of *reigi* (courtesy), about politeness and etiquette and how Tomita's failure to ask O-Sensei's permission to teach was an example of impoliteness and bad behavior. O-Sensei went so far as to say that the reason that a boy had died on the Aikido mats was because someone didn't have the right attitude toward Aikido. It probably was true that the ultimate reason that some student landed on his neck in an Aikido class was that the teacher there wasn't teaching true Aikido but something more like a fighting art.

O-Sensei turned to me and asked for my ukemi. I was just about as scared as I had ever been in my life. It reminded me once when I was in a bullring when a bull was released into it. If O-Sensei wanted to express that quality of anger and power, I was as good as dead. However, he threw me more lightly than ever. It was much lighter than he had ever done before, and he kind of beamed at me; it was almost like he was saying, "I am the master of Aikido, that means I am a master of myself."

ROBERT FRAGER

When I was uchi deshi to O-Sensei, everyone was required to wear a hakama for practice, beginning with the first time they stepped on the mat. There were no restrictions on the type of hakama you could wear then, so the dojo was a very colorful place. One saw hakama of all sorts, all colors, and all qualities, from Kendo hakama, to the striped hakama used in Japanese dance, to the costly silk hakama called *sendai hira*. I imagine that some beginning student caught the devil for borrowing his grandfather's expensive hakama, meant to be worn only for special occasions and ceremonies, and wearing out its knees in suwariwaza practice.

I vividly remember the day that I forgot my hakama. I was preparing to step on the mat for practice, wearing only my *dogi* (keikogi, training unform), when O-Sensei stopped me.

"Where is your hakama?" he demanded sternly. "What makes you think you can receive your teacher's instruction wearing nothing but your underwear? Have you no sense of propriety? You are obviously lacking the attitude and etiquette necessary in one who pursues budo training. Go sit on the side and watch class!"

This was only the first of many scoldings I was to receive from O-Sensei. However, my ignorance on this occasion prompted O-Sensei to lecture his uchi deshi after class on the meaning of the hakama. He told us that the hakama was traditional garb for *kobudo* (traditional or ancient budo) students and asked if any of us knew the reason for the seven pleats in the hakama. "They symbolize the seven virtues of budo," O-Sensei said, "These are *jin* (benevolence), *gi* (honor), *rei* (courtesy), *chi* (wisdom), *shin* (sincerity), *chu* (loyalty), and *koh* (piety). We find these qualities in the distinguished samurai of the past. The hakama prompts us to reflect on the nature of true Bushido. Wearing it symbolizes traditions that have been passed down to us from generation to generation. Aikido is born of the Bushido spirit of Japan, and in our practice we must strive to polish the seven traditional virtues."

MITSUGI SAOTOME

One time a couple of people came to watch an Aikido class. This wasn't too unusual, but these particular people were watching with an arrogant posture and sneers on their faces. This kind of irreverence made O-Sensei angry and he immediately threw them out of the dojo. He had no tolerance for disrespect of this kind.

ROBERT FRAGER

When O-Sensei spoke, students all sat in seiza humbly, like a bunch of retainers of the feudal lord, and listened to what he said. He never talked about technique. But no one could understand what he was talking about. Sometimes O-Sensei was alone at night and didn't have anyone to talk to. At these times, O-Sensei would call me over, but I ran away.

YUUICHI NAKAGUCHI

When I visited Japan, I trained at Hombu Dojo. O-Sensei was very nice to me. Every morning O-Sensei looked for me; if I wasn't training, O-Sensei would ask after me.

One morning I wasn't in class because I had too much to drink the night before and was sick in bed. O-Sensei, not seeing me in class, asked after me and learned that I was sick in bed. Understanding the nature of the illness without being told, O-Sensei came down to my room. I was in bed when O-Sensei came in, and I was so embarrassed that the founder was standing in my room that I hid under the covers. O-Sensei looked at me and said, "Why did you come to Japan? Did you come here to drink? Don't drink so much from now on."

SHIN'ICHI SUZUKI

O-Sensei didn't correct a student's hand and foot positions in class. Either people could absorb his teaching or they couldn't.

It is not like the children's class, where the teacher takes their hands and shows them in detail how to move.

YUUICHI NAKAGUCHI

O-Sensei was not a teacher of technique. You learned on a different level. You had to bring yourself to the point where you could appreciate what he was trying to teach and the way he was presenting himself in what he said.

VIRGINIA MAYHEW

Once a senior instructor complained about a newer student, saying that the student understood the hands but not the feet. The senior instructor concluded that if this student couldn't understand both, he wouldn't be able to get the movement at all. To this O-Sensei said, "Oh well, then just do the hands."

YUUICHI NAKAGUCHI

One time I asked O-Sensei in conversation if I could experience his Aikido. O-Sensei responded with dead silence.

Six months later, after I got my shodan, the moment I had put a hakama on, O-Sensei started using me as uke in class. Whenever I was in morning class, O-Sensei would come out. He would always use me as uke to demonstrate in those classes. So that was one answer, which was, if you are a white belt, you don't know where your hands and feet go and you can't be trusted to take ukemi.

ROBERT FRAGER

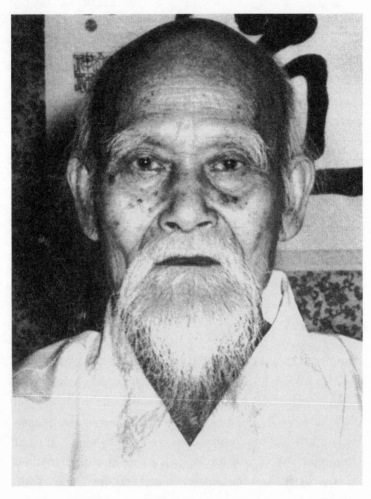

You could feel O-Sensei's power even when he wasn't doing Aikido techniques.

When I was thirteen years old, living in the Japanese country-side, O-Sensei invited me to study Aikido. He would throw down several young men simultaneously and say, "You see? This is breath." I was totally confused by his statement, because he didn't show any of his breath.

I recently realized that O-Sensei was collecting everyone's energies—positive and negative—unifying them in an extremely intense way and moving his body just a little bit to throw down people who were much larger than himself. O-Sensei, called the art he had created "Aikido," or "unifying-breath-way."

KAZUAKI TANAHASHI

O-Sensei was a completely happy person on the mat; he was very relaxed and aware. He had the skill of being able to communicate with people; he had a very special charisma. When O-Sensei came into the dojo, the entire dojo atmosphere would change; he was like a very strong force field. Sometimes O-Sensei would come and he'd be very serious. Everybody naturally noticed he was there and straightened up and became still; his presence had this kind of force to it. I think it was a spiritual connection. Of course, someone who is a very highly respected person and who is elderly summons a deeply respectful attitude in people. You can't have a sloppy attitude around someone like this. O-Sensei manifested this kind of influential presence or energy.

MITSUGI SAOTOME

O-Sensei's presence was powerful. I could tell when I walked into the dojo whether or not O-Sensei was away on a trip. It felt as though someone had the light dimmed down at Hombu Dojo. It would just be dimmer and darker. Then, all of a sudden, I would come in and it would be sparkling! This happened more than once, and I would say, "Is O-Sensei back?" and inevitably someone would say, "Yeah, he got back last night." That happened over and over again—it happened a dozen times. It was clear to me in a way that he *was* Aikido. There is one Aikido master and the rest of us are trying to figure out what he was trying to teach us.

ROBERT FRAGER

O-Sensei was always aware of his position in space. He was so close; always he came so close to getting hit by a bokken or jo; his timing was exquisite.

KAZUAKI TANAHASHI

I remember O-Sensei facing his best students with the sword and saying, "Faster, faster; come with more power; hit harder." No one was fast or strong enough for him. No matter how fast one attacked O-Sensei, he never said, "Wait a minute, that's too much."

YUUICHI NAKAGUCHI

You could feel O-Sensei's power even when he wasn't doing Aikido technique. As far as O-Sensei was concerned, being attacked by two or three people didn't even amount to an attack, he had to have at least five or six people and then he considered it something worth dealing with.

GUJI MUNETAKA KUKI

O-Sensei would visit Kumano Hongu Taisha, go to Nachi, and afterward read a book. Sometimes he would get up around two o'clock in the morning and say, "I'm going to do keiko."

One day when he was practicing with me, the tip of O-Sensei's sword broke off. "Enough," he said. I looked for the tip of O-Sensei's sword. "What are you looking for? Was it this?" asked O-Sensei, as he pulled out the sword tip from his keikogi top. It was mysterious. I could not figure out how the sword tip got into O-Sensei's keikogi.

MICHIO HIKITSUCHI

All of O-Sensei's teachings were important. O-Sensei wasn't all talk. He showed his lessons through movement. For example, he showed how to lead through iriminage. He said that in order to lead people you have to go first. In iriminage you do not pull the person toward you, but you yourself go behind them. To be a leader, you actually have to be willing to go first.

MORIHIRO SAITO

O-Sensei would show about thirty techniques in an hour. It was so fast. One student confesses that they couldn't remember so many techniques. O-Sensei would say, "Forget the techniques. You mustn't memorize them."

SHINGENOBU OKUMURA

In practice, O-Sensei taught us to look at your partner's ki. To see your partner's ki is to see the whole of your partner. Seeing in this way enables you to absorb your partner's mind, even his appearance from head to toe. It's difficult. You cannot wait for the partner to attack. You have to have the ability to perceive quickly your partner's *suki* (openings), his intent to attack.

MICHIO HIKITSUCHI

When O-Sensei taught class, he didn't teach a set thing but taught spontaneously. The custom in the dojo was that the senior student threw the junior student right and left and then the junior threw the senior right and left. However, O-Sensei would change the technique so fast that I would get thrown and when it was my turn to throw, O-Sensei would change the technique so I would get thrown again. This happened over and over.

MORIHIRO SAITO

O-Sensei got mad at me one time. This Japanese guy and I would train after O-Sensei's morning class. We just liked one another and we'd go over, and get bokken. He'd get a bokken, I'd get a bokken. We'd start fooling around by ourselves. And then, gradually, we'd start fooling with each other. Pretty soon, we'd be clacking bokken. O-Sensei came in—he'd gone out to his place and he'd come back to the dojo. When he saw what we were doing, he had us sit down. "Listen," he said, "I wish you wouldn't do that. What happens when two inexperienced people start clubbing away at each other with bokken is that somebody gets hurt. It's not that anybody means to do harm.

But things get faster and more furious, and pretty soon someone has a broken finger, or a broken nose, or worse. So please don't do that!" We agreed not to do it again.

The next morning he found us doing the same thing. O-Sensei came over and said, "I don't know if you remember what I told you yesterday, but," and he then repeated what he had said the day before. Again we sincerely agreed not to do it.

But the next morning, we were back at it. The other guy was just as dumb as I was. We agreed that we'd just go back and forth in slow motion, so there wouldn't be any sound. But we got involved in it, got going faster and faster, and eventually started clacking bokken. O-Sensei heard us, and then we heard him screaming all the way from his room, "Yeeeeeee." It was terrifying. He came running into the dojo. By the time he got to the dojo, we were both prostrate. He said that, while he realized that he had two real dumbos on his hands, he wanted to make his point anyway. So he yelled at us. Both of us felt lower than low, and dumber than dumb. I knew that he would absolutely never hurt me. But it was more terrifying than if he did. So, how do you describe somebody with such tremendous range? He could access all sorts of different stages within that process.

The next morning, after the early class, I went one way and the other guy went the other. You can bet we never swung bokken at one another again.

TERRY DOBSON

There was no weapons training at Aikikai Hombu Dojo. Once when I was just a new shodan, I was in the mat room, and when I picked up a bokken, O-Sensei came out. O-Sensei would watch what was going on from the back, so students would never know if they were being watched or not. He looked at me with his eyes and basically he said, "Don't pick it up if you don't know how to use it."

O-Sensei taught weapons to his uchi deshi, but he was not in favor of people training with weapons publicly or in open classes. However, O-Sensei never explained why. I think that his reason might be illustrated by another incident.

Once he taught me a little *kotodama* (a spiritual practice using words or voiced sounds). He taught me how to use "su" and some of the other syllables. O-Sensei turned to me and said, "Don't teach that to everyone. That can make people really strong, you could build power . . ." and he said not everybody should have it.

ROBERT FRAGER

One incident stands out from all others in my memories of this time. It happened shortly before O-Sensei went into the hospital. I can still see the Founder standing in front of me. As I faced him, my bokken poised to attack, the diminutive, frail old man was gone. In his place I saw a formidable mountain. His presence was awesome and his vibration filled the dojo. I looked into his eyes and was arrested by the powerful gravity of his spirit. The light shining there contained the wisdom and power of the ages. My body would not move. The palms of my hands were set as I gripped the wooden practice sword, and sweat was breaking out on my face. My heart pounded and I could feel its rhythm throbbing through the veins in my arms and legs. O-Sensei commanded, "Attack!" I gathered all my will into one kiai, one shout of supreme effort, attacking with all the speed and power I could muster. There was a flash of movement in front of me, and O-Sensei disappeared. I had made one fully committed strike. In the same timing, O-Sensei had evaded my strike, and I heard the whistle of his bokken cutting three times. He was standing behind me. "Saotome, you attack so slowly." Just ten minutes earlier, I had supported a weak old man laboriously up two flights of stairs and into the dojo.

MITSUGI SAOTOME

One time O-Sensei did [a technique] about twenty times while we sat watching. Then he said, "I think I'd better stop because if I do one more, you might find out what I am doing." He did one more, and then he stopped. But he added, "I don't have to worry, I still have 9,985." And that clouded the whole thing. Everything he had said before was obliterated.

HENRY KONO

Once, when I was practicing jo with O-Sensei, I thought, "What would happen if I hit him on the head with the jo right now?" At precisely that moment, O-Sensei looked at me with a very severe glance.

Another time, when O-Sensei was very sick, and the uchi deshi had to help him take off his hakama, I was behind O-Sensei, and I thought, "What would happen if I hit him right now?" Immediately O-Sensei turned around and looked at me with the same very severe glance.

Another uchi deshi tried to ambush O-Sensei in an alley that he passed through every day at a certain time. The student hid behind a wall, armed with his jo. At the usual time, he

Even as an old man, when O-Sensei stepped on the mat he became a formidable swordsman—even his senior students were not fast enough for him.

heard O-Sensei's footsteps, but then O-Sensei suddenly stopped and turned back. The student abandoned his plans. Nobody ever knew why O-Sensei had changed his routine.

NOBUYOSHI TAMURA

One day in early spring, I was teaching my English class at a Lutheran Missionary School. I was about one and one half hour's train ride outside Tokyo. The day began as a regular spring day. But it soon became cold and overcast and it started to snow in the late morning. The snow quickly became heavy—heavy enough that they dismissed classes and sent everyone home around noon.

I started back on the train to go to Hombu Dojo. I got part-way and took the subway. But then both the train and subway stopped and nothing was moving. So I started walking to Hombu Dojo in the snow. It seemed to take me one and a half hours of walking through the snow. But I persisted. It was Wednesday, and Arikawa Sensei taught a three o'clock in the afternoon Aikido class. I really liked Arikawa Sensei, and so I was motivated to get to Hombu Dojo to take his class. I didn't want to miss it.

I finally arrived at Hombu Dojo in time for his three o'clock class. But Arikawa Sensei didn't make it because of the snow. So Fugita Sensei left his post in the office to teach the class. The only other participants in the class were a group of women who were members of a Kyoto School Aikido Club. They were there for a gasshuku, and so they were staying at the dojo and taking classes. The only other student who managed to make it through the snow was one Japanese fellow.

Fugita Sensei started off the class and we were training. Then suddenly O-Sensei appeared. He had a scroll with him.

He threw Fugita around a bit and then he sat down and opened the scroll and read from it.

It was the story of Izanami and Izanagi from the *Kojiki* (the story of how the world began through the creative powers of this sister and brother, female and male). And then O-Sensei thanked—very sincerely and warmly—the women for coming so far to study Aikido. He said he hoped they would always continue to study Aikido even after they were married. He said that he also hoped that they would practice Aikido within their marriage.

For me it was a kind of nurturance, a nectar that kept me going in my training; I often felt little validation or understanding for my training in Aikido. That, plus other things that O-Sensei had said, made me believe that he valued women's participation in Aikido and that women could do Aikido.

MARY HEINY

I never saw a difference between the way O-Sensei treated women and the way he treated men.

VIRGINIA MAYHEW

O-Sensei's hands were huge—immense hands, for a man twice his size. He had long, beautiful fingers. And he had the power to hurt you with his hands. I was a big marine and so I was pretty hard to hurt. Also, my nature led me into rough activities of many kinds. Pain didn't bother me. One time O-Sensei put a *yonkyo* on me. It was something completely different from anything I'd ever felt. It felt like a red hot wire had gone across my arm. I think he understood my nature and thought I would appreciate the power of Aikido.

TERRY DOBSON

A master of his own art, O-Sensei was natural and supremely powerful. However, he also had an aura of gentleness about him.

After one morning class at Hombu dojo and after everyone else had left, I decided to take a cold, cold shower as a kind of misogi practice. When O-Sensei heard the sound of the water running, he came into the shower room and asked, "Who is there?" Then he saw me. "What are you doing, Saotome?" "Misogi! I'm training!" I answered. The shower looked like a waterfall. O-Sensei said, "But, it's cold outside, you must keep warm!"

O-Sensei had done a lot of hard misogi training, but at this time in his life, he said there was no reason to practice cold water misogi. He thought it was unnecessary to do this to your body, because it might damage it. Especially, in the cold, you must take care to keep warm.

O-Sensei did many forms of hard misogi in his lifetime. However, later in his life, when I was a student, he didn't think these practices were necessary or useful. He believed it was the function of Aikido keiko to provide the necessary misogi for Aikido students.

Many students would go to other places to do Zen training or to learn some other keiko. O-Sensei was not happy with them. But he never said anything publicly about it. Still, he said that Aikido was misogi, and so if a student wanted to train hard, they didn't need to run around learning many different things. This would be to miss the point of Aikido. "This is a *shugyo* (severe training)." O-Sensei always said, "I give you all things. Why are people always looking for other things?"

MITSUGI SAOTOME

O-Sensei always had a sword in his hand. The first time I saw O-Sensei I thought he was old. But when I tried to grab his wrist, it was like grabbing a pine tree trunk. However, he had an incredible aura of gentleness about him. He was not one to injure a student. He had an atmosphere of love. You could just feel this when you were around O-Sensei. People were not drawn so much by the technique or strength as they were by O-Sensei's character itself.

YUUICHI NAKAGUCHI

I had been living and training in Japan for a while. One day I said to myself, "I'm gonna go to Hombu and get myself a *nidan* (second-degree black belt) or a *sandan* (third-degree black belt) so that I can train really hard and push myself." I was shodan at the time. At Hombu dojo you are paired with the same person for the whole class hour; there's no switching. So, who you sit next to in the line is who you were going to get paired with. So, I was looking for where to sit; I really wanted to push my edge.

Virginia Mayhew, another American student in Japan, came over. Virginia was queen of the foreigners. She was a very sweet lady, one of the three people who founded the New York Aikikai. They had brought Yamada Sensei over from Japan to teach in New York City. And, relieved of teaching, she traveled to Japan to master Aikido. She was a very dedicated, very sincere student. She came up to me with this white belt foreigner who had just come to town. He had a new keikogi on, and she said to me, "Bob, this is Burt. Burt just started Aikido in Australia a few months ago. He came in at four o'clock this morning." Burt had been training a couple of days a week for a few months. Burt knew no Japanese and he didn't have the slightest idea of what kind of training went on at Hombu dojo. In addition, he was jet lagged. Mayhew left him with me and went off to train with a nidan or a sandan.

I look regretfully at this Burt. This was the day I was to push myself, the day I was looking for a training partner that would push me, the day I was to break through to a higher level of training. This was a real moment of truth in my life, and so several thoughts ran through my mind. Either I can ignore Burt and let the Japanese train with him and hope that he doesn't get killed before he realizes he's not ready to train here, or, I could train with Burt for somewhere between five and ten minutes and exhaust him and then train with someone else. I supposed I could tire him out without hurting him and then I could train with a nidan or sandan. But I decided to train with him; after all, Burt had come all the way from Australia to train. So, here were Burt and I, moving slowly through the forms and, next to us, were these high-stepping nidans and sandans, moving like incredible fireworks with beautiful ukemi flying all over. I was consciously trying to give Burt a good workout; pushing him beyond where he would be really comfortable, without causing injury.

At this point, O-Sensei walks into the dojo and everyone stops training and sits in seiza. Everything stops. O-Sensei gives a speech, which he commonly gives about how no one is doing Aikido properly, how they are missing the point, not understanding what Aikido is about. O-Sensei continued, "Nobody in here was trying to cooperate! Nobody in here was doing Aikido properly, except for Bob," and he pointed at me. I could've been knocked over by a feather. It was one of the greatest gifts that he had ever given me really, because he told me that Aikido is not about flashy techniques. All the stuff that

I wanted to do that day was the stuff he was hollering about. I believe that O-Sensei saw everything: that I wanted to work out with a nidan; that I really wanted to do that fast-paced, flashy technique; that I could've beaten up Burt, but that I chose not to; and, that I chose to work absolutely focused on Burt, doing the best work I could with him with as much awareness of him as possible. I am sure he saw all of that.

ROBERT FRAGER

Often when O-Sensei prayed he would be holding a jo vertically. In Shinto, this is like putting up a spiritual antenna to connect with another world.

3

DAILY
LIVING

AIKIDO IS SO VAST THAT A LIFETIME CAN BE SPENT STUDYING IT WITHOUT seeing the end of it. O-Sensei was so extraordinary, he *was* Aikido, and it's not just his *waza* (techniques), he was Aikido. There is a famous saying out of the Hassidic tradition where they ask one young Hassidic student, "Why do you go every week? Every Friday you leave work and you walk for five hours to the neighboring village to see a teacher and then every Sunday you walk five hours back. Do you go to see such an incredible master of scriptures?" "No." "Well, because he has great healing powers?" "No." "Well, why?" "I go to watch him tie his shoes." And that was the same with O-Sensei. You'd go just to watch O-Sensei put on his hakama. In his everyday life, he was Aikido.

ROBERT FRAGER

O-Sensei was concerned about the status of human life in the world and he would mostly converse about this topic. But he had a very lighthearted personality and talked easily to everybody, and he was very nonjudgmental. So it was easy to talk to him. But he never spoke about politics at all; he really wasn't interested in that.

GUJI MUNETAKA KUKI

What I find remarkable was the simplicity of O-Sensei's life. O-Sensei trained in the morning, went home, taught students at night and trained in the evening, took a bath, and went to bed. Two times a month there were special ceremonies that students would participate in, but O-Sensei would usually stay after and practice prayers in private, at the shrine and at the dojo, because the dojo also had an altar. Other than that, there was little traveling, just farming. His life was so focused; he was not distracted by fishing or listening to music or radio or reading. His focus in his art came from his life.

KAZUAKI TANAHASHI

O-Sensei got up very early in the morning when he was old. First he washed his face with water and then prayed in front of the *kamidana* (household alter). He would often go up on the roof to pray to the rising sun. Then he peeked inside the dojo to see if anyone had shown up yet. He didn't need to be at the practice all the time. Depending on who was there, he might stay one hour or only thirty minutes. After the practice, he would have breakfast—a very simple meal. He would sweep and clean and in the afternoon he would peek in the dojo, and if someone came, then he might start a practice or just start talking about something. He also read books.

SADATERU ARIKAWA

One time I told O-Sensei that the foreign students wanted to get together to wish him a happy birthday. O-Sensei thought the idea of a party was great, and he said, "Come around the back at three o'clock." One foreign student's girlfriend baked a cake. We had a really nice talk with O-Sensei. We just sat and asked questions and talked with him.

HENRY KONO

O-Sensei was a very kind grandpa who would do sumo and watch television with me. We would also go to the movies. O-Sensei's favorites were period films.

MORITERU UESHIBA DOSHU

Religion was O-Sensei's main interest. Always, he would go out to pray somewhere.

SHINGENOBU OKUMURA

One afternoon in Iwama, O-Sensei and I were watching the weekly Japanese samurai television program. O-Sensei didn't say much about technique. It was a typical samurai drama in which a lot of bad guys get chopped up. After that, we watched a Western that was dubbed in Japanese. There was a hero, a villain, and a hired gun for the villain. At the very end of the movie the hired gun steps in front of the hero and takes the bullet and dies. O-Sensei was so upset! He said, "You see, this is the problem with the West—violence!"

Surprised that O-Sensei would be upset at this single death when twice as many were killed in the samurai movie, I asked, "O-Sensei do you know how many people died in the half-hour samurai flick? Twice as many of them." But they didn't count. In the samurai movie, the deaths were faceless; they were characters you didn't know; just there to show off the hero's sword style. But the Western movie had developed the characters so that you had some attachment to them before they were killed before you. O-Sensei saw this as much more violent.

ROBERT FRAGER

O-Sensei had a very light, cheerful personality.

GUJI MUNETAKA KUKI

After WWII, when O-Sensei traveled around to teach, a student would go with him. That student would have responsibilities of helping O-Sensei—for instance in folding his hakama. When I traveled with O-Sensei after the war, meat was hard to get in Japan. But at the military police academy the meal was almost all meat. There was lots of meat for the military. At that time, O-Sensei was a vegetarian, so when we ate at the military

police academy, he would offer his portion of meat to me to eat
and I would have two people's portions of meat.

SHINGENOBU OKUMURA

O-Sensei had a simple kind of approach. He would eat anything and enjoy what he was eating. He loved *udon* (noodles)
and *manju* (Japanese sweets). He never decorated himself. He
never wore fancy clothes or anything.

GUJI MUNETAKA KUKI

O-Sensei didn't rush. He just moved around as the mood hit
him. He ate rice of course and usually one side dish, fish or
something with a pickle. When O-Sensei was invited to a ban-
quet, he ate almost nothing; little suited him. The Ueshiba
family had a simple life and ate simple food.

SADATERU ARIKAWA

O-Sensei would eat chicken and eggs (eggs were a real treat
after WWII!), but he would not eat the meat of four-legged an-
imals. People mostly ate sweet potatoes. After O-Sensei ate his
first small bowl of rice, his wife would say, "Would you like
some more?" He would say, "Yes, give me three more grains"—
meaning that he would just eat a little bit more.

KAZUAKI TANAHASHI

O-Sensei was old when I became his pupil. To look at him, you
wouldn't think it, but he was very strong. Another thing that
impressed me about him was his generosity. When we would

have tea together, he would offer half of his *okashi* (a Japanese snack) saying, "You, eat!"

MAMORU SUGANUMA

O-Sensei never said, "No." He always said "Yes." He was very accommodating to people . . . all day. He could just really deal with any circumstance and he was OK with it.

GUJI MUNETAKA KUKI

O-Sensei had a tremendously generous spirit, and he always wanted to give everything away to other people. Even something that was very precious to him he would immediately give to people if they wanted it.

GUJI YUKITAKA YAMAMOTO

O-Sensei would come to my father's house in Tokyo when I was twelve or thirteen. I did go to the dojo in Tokyo and to the Iwama dojo, but I never trained. I thought O-Sensei was just a magnificent person.

GUJI MUNETAKA KUKI

O-Sensei always called himself *ji*, old man. "As for this old man," he used to say. O-Sensei would change his voice and use of language in a formal situation. This was the case of people born before the war.

SADATERU ARIKAWA

Farming and just being with nature are ways of offering prayers to a higher realm. O-Sensei's farming was part of his practice. He was a very skillled and powerful farmer.

O-Sensei taught an evening class, and that would be the extent of most people's contact with him. However, he would teach off and on during the day and then sit and have tea. Live-in students were fortunate to be able to listen to O-Sensei. He told us many wonderful things.

MORIHIRO SAITO

O-Sensei loved being in the dojo and talking to people. Many people came to talk to him. He always seemed to have a lot of older women coming to speak to him. These women were not Aikido students; some were neighbors. People who loved to talk about spiritual matters came by to talk to him.

SADATERU ARIKAWA

Once a man who was a smoker offered O-Sensei a cigarette. O-Sensei threw it away. Then the man put his hands together and apologized to O-Sensei.

YUUICHI NAKAGUCHI

O-Sensei was relaxed, but he never sat cross-legged; he was always in seiza. He would read books and talk; he always talked of spiritual matters. After he was seventy years old, he rarely drank; he would only drink a little sake on special occasions.

MICHIO HIKITSUCHI

After evening practice, O-Sensei would retire to his house and have some students do shiatsu on him. Sometimes three would do it at once. He would strengthen his muscles by pushing against the three poor students trying to do shiatsu, and their hands and muscles would become very tired.

MORIHIRO SAITO

Tokyo was always the stopping point on O-Sensei's travels. He would start in Iwama and come first to Tokyo and get energy and take care of some affairs and then go on to Osaka or Wakayama. Then he would stop by Tokyo on the way back to Iwama.

SADATERU ARIKAWA

Traveling to O-Sensei's country dojo in Iwama required a two-hour train ride from Tokyo station. One day I was traveling with O-Sensei to stay a couple of days in Iwama. It's not a big deal to go to Iwama; you take the train there and walk to the dojo from the train station. But when O-Sensei went, someone had to go with him. So this time I went with him.

I was the only one there with him. I met his wife and they had a servant girl, who was from the country and who worked for them. They had something that was more than a garden, it was like a small farm in the back of the dojo. There were quite a lot of plants. It was amazing.

It was hot, it was summer, it was really hot. His wife would go, "Well, I think I will go out and talk to the plants." She would walk out in the heat of the day, and she'd weed and water. To her it wasn't any big deal; but I could barely move in that heat. I was exhausted and tired and hot and I just thought it was amazing that she would go out there and be weeding.

ROBERT FRAGER

After the war, food was rationed. People got coupons they exchanged for food. O-Sensei said he wasn't going to do that and that he would grow his own food. Here he could only grow enough food for his family, because he spent the morning praying and training. There wasn't much time left for fieldwork.

MORIHIRO SAITO

After the war, the only structure left standing in this whole area (Shinjuku) was Aikikai Hombu Dojo. All else was burned from incendiary bombs. O-Sensei's son, Kisshomaru, fought to save the house. Thirteen families were then living in the Ueshiba house. When I returned, three years after the war's end, there were still about three or four families living there.

There were no classes then. There wasn't any food. No one had any energy. People tried to grow some sweet potatoes to eat. When we did train, we trained on wood, because there was no tatami. O-Sensei was growing food in Iwama, which he would often bring down. Of course, if I went up to Iwama, I could get some potatoes or vegetables. There was no food in Tokyo.

SHINGENOBU OKUMURA

The Founder was a prominent member of the community, and he had the distinction of having the only electricity in the area.

MORIHIRO SAITO

O-Sensei's farming was part of his practice. Much earlier, O-Sensei farmed when he created the community of Shirataki in Hokkaido. After WWII, food was scarce in the city, and O-Sensei knew he could feed people if he farmed. So, he increased the fields in Iwama and farmed a lot.

SHINGENOBU OKUMURA

A few years after the end of the war, life began to return to normal. The country was still in transition, and there were many people without jobs. Many joined the Iwama dojo looking for a new chance at life. Although O-Sensei had a garden at the dojo, there were soon more mouths to feed than he could handle. O-Sensei put the new uchi deshi to work clearing nearby fields so that they could be planted. Although O-Sensei had his students clear bamboo fields to make more space for growing vegetables, this practice was not typical for dojos.

MORIHIRO SAITO

O-Sensei was very powerful; when he was farming, he was amazing. His way of breathing was to go, "Sh, sh, sh." He was exhaling with sound, and working with great vigor, very fast. He was a very skilled farmer.

KAZUAKI TANAHASHI

O-Sensei had a couple of students, one was Oyama, who was a wrestler and a huge man. During the rice harvest, all the students were helping to harvest the rice, including Oyama. To harvest rice, you climb down into the paddy and cut and tie the stalks into bundles and carry them up and out of the paddy.

This was very heavy work, climbing out of the paddy with water-soaked stalks. But no one—not even Oyama—could match O-Sensei even at sixty-three years old.

MORIHIRO SAITO

Uchi deshi were always collecting the dead branches for fires. O-Sensei didn't like cutting branches for fires. He wanted dead branches for the fire, so there was no waste. Also, he would have the ash saved to help make a good compost with other vegetable wastes. He would use it on his garden.

MITSUGI SAOTOME

Students who lived with O-Sensei in Iwama took care of the farm in order to eat. O-Sensei was very energetic, and he used heavier agriculture tools that were specially made for him. When O-Sensei carried something, he carried a staff twice as heavy as those the students carried.

MORIHIRO SAITO

One day O-Sensei said to me, "Saotome, that stone step must be moved a little closer to the house; it's difficult to step inside." Looking at the six-foot-long, one-foot-square solid piece of marble that my teacher had indicated, I knew it was too heavy for two men to move. I had returned from the tool shed and was rigging up a makeshift lever when I heard O-Sensei behind me. "Saotome, what are you doing?" Impatiently he pushed me out of his way and grasped one end of the marble slab. With a small grunt he lifted it and moved it over the necessary six inches. He then went to the other end and, following the same procedure,

*O-Sensei could stop a person with just a glance. His
eyes were very expressive; his look could be so stern at
one moment that arrows seemed to fly from his eyes.*

completed the task. I stood staring, open-mouthed, as he mumbled in a disgusted voice. "Modern boys are so weak!" I was in my early twenties, and my muscles were strong and well tuned from many hours each day of hard Aikido training. But I could not budge the marble step that the four-foot-ten, seventy-eight-year-old master of Aikido had so easily moved.

MITSUGI SAOTOME

O-Sensei was unbelievably strong. He did so many amazing things. His great strength remains in my memory.

MORIHIRO SAITO

O-Sensei had an amazing body. He looked like a partition screen (square shape) when he was fifty-three years old. He weighed about 150 kilograms. He was 150 centimeters tall and was very wide. It was a body of strong joints and bones. Of course, he had a mustache. He was strongly built and full of vigor. His gaze was very kind, but he also had a fierce light in them as though they were glowing. It was intimidating! If he looked at you suddenly, you were frozen, unable to move.

MICHIO HIKITSUCHI

I remember that O-Sensei's eyes would glitter and shine. Everyone will say that O-Sensei's eyes were special.

MORIHIRO SAITO

O-Sensei was a great *budo-ka* (student of Budo), an amazing budo-ka. I was afraid to be next to him and yet I felt he had a benevolent, kindly heart. He was fearsome, and yet I was drawn to him. I did feel his physical strength. With just a glance from him, I felt as though I had been shot with an arrow. His glance could be so stern at one moment and soft and kindly the next. I felt he was my own parent. He looked stern and his body was so strong and yet, when I came nearby I felt that here sat a genuinely kind person.

MICHIO HIKITSUCHI

I used to judge how to approach O-Sensei according to the state of his eyes (gaze). I couldn't stare at O-Sensei's eyes, because it is rude to stare at someone's eyes. So I would look in a general way toward O-Sensei, as though I were looking at a huge mountain behind O-Sensei and then I could catch how O-Sensei's eyes looked.

SADATERU ARIKAWA

O-Sensei always stared sharply at someone he was meeting for the first time. His eyes gleamed. In that moment O-Sensei knew everything about that person.

MICHIO HIKITSUCHI

From his deathbed, O-Sensei looked up and indicated that he wanted to go to the bathroom. "I'm sorry, but after lying in bed all day this old man's legs are very weak." I quickly took one arm, and my close friend Yoshio Kuriowa took the other. Slowly we proceeded down the hall, holding him tight lest he fall and injure himself. O-Sensei suddenly straightened, pride flashing in his eyes. "I don't need any help." With a powerful shudder of his body, he freed his arms from our grasp. The weakened and dying old man had thrown two master instructors. Our bodies flew until we pounded into the walls on either side. Step by step Morihei Ueshiba made his way alone. With each step his life was burning like the last brilliant flare of a candle before its fire disappears. Calm and at peace in the face of his approaching death, he seized the reality of each moment as it occurred. There was only that moment; each breath was infinity. How many memories did each step contain?

MITSUGI SAOTOME

O-Sensei was willing to really relate with anybody. He didn't say, "Oh, that's a bad person, I won't have anything to do with them," or, "This is a good person, I'll stick with them." He was very accepting of human beings.

GUJI MUNETAKA KUKI

In a Japanese fairy tale, there were two old men. One always behaved in a warm and friendly fashion and had the ability to make the trees bloom. The other was meanspirited and couldn't make the trees bloom. O-Sensei was like the kindly old man who could make the trees bloom. In Japan, we call this *"kokoji."*

SADATERU ARIKAWA

As time went on, I just became more and more impressed with O-Sensei's capacity to encompass and surround everything; a hugeness of spirit. O-Sensei was an amazing person who was always at ease with himself and able to speak on any subject freely without holding himself back.

GUJI MUNETAKA KUKI

O-Sensei was very devout. Whenever he passed a shrine, he clasped his hands together and said a silent prayer. O-Sensei was a strict teacher, but also he was very kind, warm, sympathetic, and magnanimous. I believe he had a deep love for all life.

MAMORU SUGANUMA

O-Sensei loved to practice calligraphy, and many people would come and ask him for a sample of his calligraphy. He'd write on a fan or on the square tablets. People would ask him to write something for them, something specific. It would be something related to budo.

SHINGENOBU OKUMURA

O-Sensei always relied on ki, kokyu, the ki of heaven, earth, and the universe, to live a moderate life. He was a magnanimous man. He had no aggression. O-Sensei didn't have an ego. He never went around with a sense of pride. He was large just like the sky.

GUJI MUNETAKA KUKI

Daily O-Sensei would get up and go to pray at the shrine. But before he went to the shrine, he would always take a bath to make his body clean. Uchi deshi were responsible for making

O-Sensei's bath ready. We were always making a hot tub of water. At this time in Iwama there was no gas, not even propane gas. O-Sensei didn't like gas anyway; he preferred the wood branch to make a natural fire. He didn't like us to take branches from living trees, so we always collected branches that were already on the ground.

Many times I prepared O-Sensei's bath. I would have to fill the tub with a pot, because there was no hose, and then collect the wood and build a fire to make the water hot. I always checked the water in the tub with my hand to make sure it wasn't too hot.

One time O-Sensei saw me checking the water in this way. O-Sensei looked at me and said, "what are you doing there, Saotome?" "Hai!" I said, "I was just checking the temperature of the hot water!" O-Sensei was so pissed off! "You know, you're foolish! I take a bath before I pray, so why would you test the water with your smoky, dirty hands?" He was so angry. "If you want to check the temperature of the water, you must scoop out a small part of the water with a dipper and then check the temperature with your hand in the dipper. Because you've put your hand in the entire bath, this water is now dirty and I can't take a bath. So one more." And I had to start all over.

Cleansing the body before praying is a very spiritual practice. So, bathing in dirty water would not be an appropriate thing to do to prepare for prayers before the shrine. Spiritual practice has very strict protocols. I have always regarded this as a very good lesson in attitude.

MITSUGI SAOTOME

O-Sensei didn't do strength-building things, but he did water misogi (pouring cold water over yourself) during both winter

O-Sensei's arm was like a piece of iron, very strong and very hard to move. But there was something besides physical strength that made him strong. He had a kind of mysterious energy, a vastness of ki that came from his contact with higher forces.

and summer. He used the well water. There was a bucket that you lowered and pulled up.

MORIHIRO SAITO

I remember O-Sensei as a person of complete integrity and sincerity. There was never any conflict between what he said and what he did. O-Sensei's sincerity inspired his followers to stick with him.

MOTOMICHI ANNO

At first after the war there was no food. O-Sensei would get up very early and pray at the shrine. Then there was class and then breakfast at ten o'clock in the morning. We would boil potatoes with the rice, because there wasn't enough rice to serve without potatoes. Then he would work in the fields for the rest of the day, except for winter. Normally people get up and go to the fields early during the cooler part of the day and rest during the hottest. But O-Sensei would use the cooler part of the day for prayers and training and start work in the field in the full heat just as the others were leaving their fields.

MORIHIRO SAITO

At night O-Sensei might be invited to teach at another dojo or sometimes he'd show up at the class. When he had a big seminar in Tokyo, he would show up early because he enjoyed seminars. O-Sensei loved practice so much that it was his joy, almost recreation more than training.

SADATERU ARIKAWA

O-Sensei didn't have other interests outside of *shodo* (brushwork), misogi, and Aikido. I accompanied O-Sensei when Hikitsuchi Sensei opened the dojo in Shingu in 1952. We stayed about three weeks, and during that time, O-Sensei would teach from five to seven o'clock in the morning every day. But after that there wasn't any training until six o'clock in the evening. Noting that there were a lot of unoccupied hours in the day between classes, O-Sensei suggested that since I was a calligrapher, that I teach calligraphy to the local children. About thirty kids came for class. O-Sensei said, "If you teach the children, they will pay you a fee and you should teach them some splendid technique in return." As I began teaching the children calligraphy, O-Sensei watched. When he watched me teach the children and saw us brushing together, his eyes were very kind. He showed an interest in it and said, "Well maybe I will do some, too."

O-Sensei and I had done calligraphy together. O-Sensei's calligraphy was already wonderful; he was skilled from an early age. When O-Sensei wrote, he put his vitality, his life force, into what he was writing. One immediately notices that even though O-Sensei's body is gone, that his incredible life force remains in his calligraphy. It is so moving because O-Sensei deliberately put his energy and life force into his calligraphy. We can understand O-Sensei's ki power that can't be seen.

The calligraphy of ordinary people basically disappears over time, but O-Sensei's won't do that. O-Sensei continues to live through his work even though his body passed away thirty-three years ago. He continues to live through his works and will fifty years from now and two hundred years from now; because unlike calligraphy masters who are popular for a period of time, O-Sensei's calligraphy will always have charm. You could write that O-Sensei is his shodo. His calligraphy and his life are the same. His life force is the shodo. They are one and the same. O-Sensei's body has become ashes and air, but O-Sensei's life continues in the calligraphy. And, as a matter of fact, O-Sensei's correct Aikido techniques continue in the calligraphy. It doesn't just continue, but it will continue to expand and blossom forever.

SEISEKI ABE

O-Sensei was often invited to the homes of the nobility.

SADATERU ARIKAWA

When O-Sensei visited the shrine, he always wore a kimono like a Japanese gentleman. O-Sensei was very stable, he was a kind of down-to-earth personality. He wasn't eccentric or anything like that. He was rather ordinary in a way.

GUJI MUNETAKA KUKI

After Japan lost WWII, the Japanese people just gave up Japanese style: clothing, swords, even general concepts. But O-Sensei was always walking in kimono and samurai clothes. He was kind of eccentric, and in a way people thought that he was anachronistic.

KAZUAKI TANAHASHI

Most of the movies taken of O-Sensei were done at the dojo, and so they don't show how O-Sensei acted in a very formal situation. But, what O-Sensei did at a public demonstration and at the dojo was different, and he very naturally adapted to each situation. It was not calculated. He always understood what to do. He could respond to the atmosphere of whatever situation he was in. In ordinary practice he smiled and was at ease. When he came into the dojo during practice, he just looked like a friendly old man. A new person might think that just a friendly old man had come in. His appearance would change according to the circumstances. O-Sensei always was alert and could assess the circumstances and match himself to them.

O-Sensei's eyes were different depending on whether he was in public or private. His eyes were different again depending on what type of public place he was in. One type of public occasion was very formal and O-Sensei would dress in a formal kimono and bow formally. Another type of occasion was less formal like when he would visit another Aikido dojo, and in such a place he would wear a less formal kimono. Usually he looked like any older person in what he wore.

SADATERU ARIKAWA

The amazing and wonderful thing about O-Sensei's ordinary life is that even when he wrote in his diary or wrote with pen, a fountain pen or ballpoint pen, the characters were just magnificent. It showed an amazing artistic capacity that O-Sensei had. The wonderful quality of O-Sensei's ordinary life can be seen in the fact that even his casual writing was splendid.

SEISEKI ABE

O-Sensei would summon me often to come and talk with him. These weren't interviews but just conversations. I lived in Hombu Dojo for more than ten years, so O-Sensei called me anytime. If I wanted to talk about something specific, I would try to change O-Sensei's pace of conversation into mine to get to the topic. To ask O-Sensei questions, I had to study a lot.

SADATERU ARIKAWA

When I was visiting Hombu Dojo and I was called into O-Sensei' office, O-Sensei wanted to talk to me about Aikido. But O-Sensei used high-class Japanese, and I didn't understand anything he was saying. Still, I wanted to be polite, so I would sit at attention and say *"hai, hai* (yes, yes)." O-Sensei mistook my respectful demeanor as understanding and agreement and continued to talk to me by the hour. I was very embarrassed when finally O-Sensei went out of the room and sternly addressed a group of his own live-in students, "I don't understand why none of you understand me when this young man from Hawaii does."

SHIN'ICHI SUZUKI

I was traveling back to Tokyo from Iwama with O-Sensei. Upon boarding the train, O-Sensei sat down next to a little old lady and said, "I'm Ueshiba of Aikido." She replied, "That's nice. What's Aikido?" And he says, "Well, it is a budo and . . ." "What's a budo?" she asks. It was clear that her world had nothing to do with budo, or Aikido, or anything like that. So O-Sensei said, "This is my deshi, Bob; he is from Harvard." And O-Sensei started talking about me much to my embarrassment. Listening from the seat nearby, I was thrown that a great man like O-Sensei would be talking about me to anyone.

As O-Sensei continued to talk to the little old lady, I realized that O-Sensei really wanted to entertain this woman on the train and that in order to do that, he needed to talk about something that she would recognize. In those years, everybody knew about Harvard, because John F. Kennedy had been from Harvard, and O-Sensei knew this. O-Sensei was entertaining her by talking about his student, because if he talked about himself, the conversation wouldn't take off. He was willing to talk about his student, which is so extraordinary; he was just extraordinary off the mat as well as on the mat. I mean, he was just amazing.

ROBERT FRAGER

When I lived at the dojo, I observed O-Sensei's daily life. I saw how O-Sensei behaved at a big seminar with important people attending and how he behaved in informal situations. I was always impressed with O-Sensei's ability to adapt to each circumstance and always behave perfectly appropriately. It didn't seem to be something O-Sensei had to think about; he just seemed taken over by the event and just naturally behaved completely correctly. O-Sensei's deportment was always correct to the situation. In some sense, O-Sensei cultivated this ability because it is a way to avoid creating enemies.

SADATERU ARIKAWA

When O-Sensei did brushwork, he put his vitality,
his lifeforce, into what he was brushing.

O-Sensei would always go early in the morning to pray. When O-Sensei prayed at the shrine, he was very dignified and serious. He was properly dressed in *haori* (a Japanese half-coat) and hakama. I accompanied him to the Kumano Hongu Taisha over one hundred times.

MICHIO HIKITSUCHI

O-Sensei started to build a small shrine outside in the grasses. The uchi deshi would go with O-Sensei when he prayed. O-Sensei would chant a long prayer, and his students would sit seiza in the grass behind him. But, as we were sitting there respectfully, mosquitoes were buzzing and biting and ants were swarming and biting. I would be so distracted I would hope O-Sensei would finish chanting soon, but he would go strong for a long time. O-Sensei had no problem with biting mosquitoes; they didn't go to him. The sounds and vibrations would keep them away.

MITSUGI SAOTOME

In Iwama, they had an old-fashioned *ofuro* (Japanese bath) the servant girl would heat up every morning. Because you heat it up with wood, she'd be up at three or four o'clock in the morning. Also, she'd put wood in the stove to cook the rice. O-Sensei and his students would get up an hour later, at five o'clock, and then make the rounds of praying at the Aikido shrine in the dojo, the main Aikido shrine, and the little shrine over there in the little farm. O-Sensei would get up and go around to each shrine and pray, reciting the Norito.

One time I was visiting Iwama with O-Sensei. When it came time to get in the ofuro, O-Sensei told me to go first. I was mortified; because in seniority I was underneath O-Sensei, and students demonstrate their respect by putting great teachers first. But O-Sensei insisted; O-Sensei had incredible humility.

ROBERT FRAGER

Once when I was traveling with O-Sensei, I made his bath for him. I got the wood, chopped it, and made the bath. It was just a cement bowl, and you make the fire under it. It's not big, I could barely get into it. The rule is always that the sensei goes first. If he even lets you have a bath, there was no question that I, being the last uchi deshi, should be last. One night I was fanning the fire. I was about to go call him and say, "Sensei, your bath is ready," and there he was.

He spoke to me as though he were speaking to a little kid. He made me take my clothes off. "Take some water," he said. I had to stand next to the bowl and clean myself before getting into the bath. I had to pour it over my head and soap up. "Now wash behind your ears, get in your ears, that's good." Just like a little kid. Then he said, "OK, get in the bath," and I sat with my knees up to my chin. I said "Yeah, it's very good." Actually, it wasn't comfortable at all. I was very embarrassed. But, he would do that sometimes. He could kill you with sweetness if he wanted to.

TERRY DOBSON

One time O-Sensei was coming up the stairs. He was older by this time, and so he was walking very slowly and deliberately stepping as he came up the stairs. As O-Sensei made his careful climb, a young boy came racing up the stairs past him, which is not a very polite thing to do in Japan. O-Sensei stopped and looked up and said, "Rude, uncivilized boy!

MASAKI TANI

O-Sensei would walk, taking off in a direction he intuitively chose. He could choose his direction according to his feeling and not according to the direction something actually was. But if one was too forceful in telling him he was going in the wrong direction, he got mad. One had to say politely, "I think we should turn right here." Then he would say, "Oh, is that right? OK then."

MORIHIRO SAITO

The first time I was allowed to be alone with O-Sensei on a long trip, I went as his bag carrier. We were going to Osaka. I knew that I was supposed to be committed enough to O-Sensei to throw myself in front of the train if need be. I was told that I had to stay with him at all times, not to get more than three feet away from him. I was told that when we were riding in the taxi, I was to have the money ready in my hands to give to the driver. I was told to jump out of the taxi and run around and open the door for O-Sensei, pay the driver, and get the bags. I felt that the job required my total concentration.

So, when we got to the station, I had the mathematics all worked out, I had the right change. I paid the driver, jumped out of the car, and leapt over to O-Sensei's side of the cab to help him out. O-Sensei got out. It was noon at the old Tokyo

Station, and it was crowded. I was determined that nobody should run into O-Sensei. You have to keep in mind that he was four foot ten and eighty years old. I would be mortified if anything happened to him. I reached into the taxi to get the bags. I had gotten the bags, and I turned around. I was looking ferocious. By the time I turned around, O-Sensei was on the sidewalk and half way to the station. I said, "Wait a minute, what did he do, fly?" I was sort of swinging these bags and running. I must have hit forty people who were trying to get out of my way. I'd hit them, and I'd have to say, "I'm sorry" and they'd say, "I'm sorry."

O-Sensei moved like a knife through soft butter. He was so small, you couldn't see him in a crowd very easily. I started to watch where the crowd opened up. I noticed that nobody looked at him, nobody saw him. I was trampling old ladies. By the time I got to where I'd first seen him, he was already at the station.

I knew what track we were going to. I caught sight of him near the staircase to the track. I knew he needed help getting up the stairs. But by the time I got to the bottom of the staircase, I could just see his head leaving at the top of the stairs. I ran up the stairs full speed and ran down the platform. I thought, "Oh, Jesus Christ, I lost him." He was hiding—not really, but it was really hard to see him. I run up, panting. He was on the platform fully a minute before I got there. He looked at me and said, "Is there some trouble?"

TERRY DOBSON

As a younger man, O-Sensei would run up the steps to the shrine; but as he aged, he wouldn't run. As a young boy, I sometimes watched from the top of the stairs as O-Sensei ascended them. Sometimes it was frightening, because he would go in his *geta* faster and faster, and as he neared the top, his eyes seemed to glow as if he were coming home.

IETAKA KUKI

When O-Sensei wanted to go to Tokyo, he took the train. However, the trains ran very infrequently, one every hour or hour and a half. O-Sensei would get up and be completely dressed way before the train was due. Suddenly, he would stand up and announce he was going even though it wasn't close to the time for the train to come. O-Sensei could move very fast. The student attending him for that day would have to be ready to go at any time. In Tokyo, where it was crowded, he would walk quickly and smoothly through the crowds, whereas the deshi who were carrying all the bags would be crashing into people and losing sight of him.

MORIHIRO SAITO

When I was with O-Sensei on long train trips, he would always sit in proper seiza and not move at all. The students would try to do the same, but it was very difficult. That's shugyo. O-Sensei would sit like that as he talked about various things. The students would have put their legs out. But O-Sensei never did move his legs.

MICHIO HIKITSUCHI

There were frequently times during traveling when O-Sensei and the student accompanying him would eat at restaurants. Before leaving, O-Sensei would often buy a small gift to give to his wife when he returned home. He was always very kind to her. She was always around, and students called her *Oku-sama* (Honorable Wife).

MAMORU SUGANUMA

All of O-Sensei's students recognized that his wife, Hatsu, was one of the main pillars in supporting Aikido. She worked as hard as O-Sensei at making Aikido a success.

SHINGENOBU OKUMURA

O-Sensei's students called O-Sensei "O-Sensei." O-Sensei means "great teacher"; "sensei" is teacher in Japanese and "O" is the honorific. O-Sensei's students called him this and thought of him in this way.

During my travels to O-Sensei's country dojo in Iwama, I was present for family meals, which would include O-Sensei's wife, Hatsu. She used a very endearing term for O-Sensei that was so intimate that I had to pretend I didn't hear it when she said it. She called him *Mori-chan*. "Chan" is what you would call a child. It is like "Mori-baby"! I would never even think of calling him by his first name, Morihei, but "Mori-chan"! It was obvious that they had this wonderfully intimate relationship.

ROBERT FRAGER

O-Sensei had no desire for material things. He was a genius and did not have ordinary perceptions about things.

SHINGENOBU OKUMURA

*O-Sensei's wife, Hatsu, sewing his garment. It was very clear
that they had a wonderfully intimate relationship. O-Sensei was
always very kind to her and she was very supportive of Aikido.*

After two years of study, I traveled with O-Sensei from Tokyo to Iwama. As soon as the train pulled out, I took the opportunity to ask O-Sensei a question, "People say that in 1926 you got ki. Is that right?" O-Sensei looked at me and requested the names of all the people who said that. O-Sensei said, "It's all a lie. You want to know something? I was born with it."

I was quiet after that. But, just before we debarked in Iwama, O-Sensei told me, "You go back to Canada. You teach Aikido. You will understand what ki is." And then O-Sensei gave me a nice smile.

HENRY KONO

I'd be talking to O-Sensei and he would suddenly say, "Somebody's coming," and then afterward somebody would come.

SHINGENOBU OKUMURA

O-Sensei had the martial arts' manner in which one is ready for anything. He never relaxed his posture, but he sat as though he were expecting a student to try to attack him at any time, even when he was sleeping.

MOTOICHI YANASE

O-Sensei was always grounded. Whether he was moving or kneeling or sitting, no imbalance was revealed, no gap, no opening. O-Sensei was always present and ready. It is a continuous kind of presence: his eyes were aware, open to the people around him whether they were attacking or not.

KAZUAKI TANAHASHI

One time I went with O-Sensei on a pilgrimage to Isei shrine and we stayed on the third floor of an inn. In the middle of the night, O-Sensei woke me up and said, "I smell gas—go tell the master of the house there is a gas leak." So I went down to the second floor, then down to the first floor, and I couldn't smell anything. Still not convinced there was any gas leak, I went into the kitchen and I looked at the pilot light; I saw that the pilot light had burnt out and gas was coming out! O-Sensei could tell from the third floor of the inn when no one else in the inn, not even the maids, could smell it. How incredibly sharp O-Sensei's senses were!

SHINGENOBU OKUMURA

Rather than talking politics or current events, O-Sensei was more of a model for people because every day of his life he lived his philosophy. He never dealt with money; he never asked for money. He had no desire for material things at all. He had no desire to accumulate anything; he just went through life clad in his warm heart. He never insisted that people really promote him or his art. But people around him tried to promote him and the art. He himself never did that.

GUJI MUNETAKA KUKI

The wonderful light in O-Sensei's eyes was the light of love; his intense desire that we cultivate Aikido.

ART
OF PEACE

O-SENSEI WAS STRICT WITH HIMSELF AND KIND TO OTHERS. ALL THE TIME O-Sensei would say that the purpose of Aikido was to become one with nature, make one's own heart the heart of nature. O-Sensei talked about the need to rid oneself of the desire to fight with the opponent, about the need to create harmony. O-Sensei would say, "Aikido is the budo of love. You must give happiness and joy to your partner. If you do that, you can become harmonious. You will be harmonious. To have a good relationship with another, you must not harbor anger. Your anger will infect your partner. That must not happen. Offer happiness. Be compassionate. If you do that mutually, you will make harmony and be like a family."

It is different today than it was before. Today, people think only of themselves. If they have power and money, they are happy and think that killing one another is OK. We must correct this. If we don't, how can we create a true family? O-Sensei said, "I am alive to make the world one family."

MICHIO HIKITSUCHI

I owe much to O-Sensei. O-Sensei was a person who liked to travel around a lot and he used to invite me to go along. For instance, when I was in Tokyo, O-Sensei would say, "Oh, tomorrow I have to go to the Igura Hot Springs. Want to come?" I would go with him. It was an incredible place! O-Sensei went there, not for the hot springs so much but because a teacher of a particular religious sect was there. After O-Sensei's visit, one of the members of the audience went to Osaka to spread the sect there; another became a priest. I think they were moved by O-Sensei's words.

GUJI MUNETAKA KUKI

O-Sensei put it quite simply: *Bu wa ai nari* (martial art or virtue is love). Budo is love. O-Sensei clearly said that Aikido is love.

SHINGENOBU OKUMURA

Because of O-Sensei's war experience, he always worried about how to stop the spear. "Stop the spear" is the true meaning of *bu*.

O-Sensei was always talking about the world's condition. He

was always praying, worrying, caring about global issues. He was concerned with why there is so much killing, so much crime and war. Twenty-four hours a day, he extended his mind to the world community, connecting to the global society.

MITSUGI SAOTOME

O-Sensei said that Aikido is not about technique, but that it is about how humans should live their lives. Aikido is not really about theory or rationalization. The spirit of Aikido is to create a sphere, a warm sphere, a warm circle of harmonious feeling among people so that people can get along with each other with warm-hearted feeling.

GUJI MUNETAKA KUKI

One of O-Sensei's sayings was: *"Kokoro maruku taisanmen ni hirake."* Kokoro is heart. The whole phrase can be translated, "When you stand in *hanmi* (an Aikido stance), have an open heart."

Another of O-Sensei's sayings was *"Uchu no ugoki wa ryo ashi ni ari, atama no hataraki wa ryote ni ari."* O-Sensei said this over and over and over. It can be translated, "The movement of nature is in the feet, the movement of strategy (or intellect) is in the hands."

HENRY KONO

O-Sensei's arm was like a piece of iron, very strong, and very hard to move. Muscularly, O-Sensei was a very strong man. But there was something besides just physical strength. There was a kind of mysterious energy that came from something else: years of training and experience from all situations. But beyond what is really amazing and outstanding and sublime was the vastness of his ki. I think it comes from his contact with higher forces and his practice of prayers and rituals and his voice, his chanting.

KAZUAKI TANAHASHI

One day we got into an accident. Our car hit the train and swung hard. All the windows were broken and the car was unable to drive. I was seriously injured, but O-Sensei did not get hurt at all because he settled ki at the time of the accident.

SEISEKI ABE

O-Sensei said Aikido is a cross within a circle. The circle symbolizes the universe, and the cross is the point in space without time. To be here now is most important. If you spend time worrying about tomorrow or yesterday, it is empty here and now.

MAMORU SUGANUMA

Ueshiba O-Sensei had a deep faith in the kami of the Kumano area from early childhood. He was born in Tanabe, which is nearby, so from a very early age, he would come to the Kumano shrine. O-Sensei used to come here every year until he died. O-Sensei often said that the techniques of Aikido were taught to him by the kami of Kumano, that Aikido was not something he set out to create but that he received Aikido from the kami of Kumano.

What I remember clearly is O-Sensei saying that the *Aiki no kami* is the Kumano kami. *Agatsu Katsuhayahi no Mikoto* is the name of a Kumano kami. "Self victory; always victorious." This phrase is actually the name of the deity. So it means there is never any defeat.

GUJI MUNETAKA KUKI

I went on a trip with O-Sensei to Kyoto for three or four days. He had almost no meetings with anybody. We stayed in this house, in rooms right next to each other. I could hear every move he made. Whatever he needed, I would provide for him. If he needed something, he would just say it through the screen and I would get it for him.

What he did during those days was pray. That's what he did. That's his point of origin. He didn't go to the movies, go out on a date, or entertain a bunch of people. He just talked to God. His truth was that he believed what he was doing was the way to reconcile the world, to bring about peace. When he wasn't doing that, he didn't reach for ego support. He was self-contained. I think that's extremely important. Throughout history, there have been people like him whose ability to deal with opposing force in miraculous ways was profound; it was extensive. That was their preaching. Just like some people are able to handle snakes without being bitten. Or others are able to heal without touching.

TERRY DOBSON

The Founder's religious beliefs really affected the art he developed. He used to say that he studied technique after prayer, with mind and body unified. So, the shrine is not just an ordinary religious place. It is a shrine to the god of budo.

MORIHIRO SAITO

People talk about the wonderful light in O-Sensei's eyes. That light was not the light of anger but the light of love. It was not a fearsome light but his intense desire that we cultivate Aikido.

MOTOMICHI ANNO

O-Sensei was able to read people's eyes and know their individual character.

SADATERU ARIKAWA

O-Sensei caused natural reverence. If O-Sensei was in front of you, your head just naturally bowed. Students didn't bow their heads out of fear, but because they felt that way in their hearts. Also, O-Sensei's eyes were so bright, they were splendid eyes. Amazing eyes, clear and beautiful. If he gazed at you suddenly, you felt stuck to the spot, frozen. He could be silent and still draw someone to him with his eyes. How was it he could draw out such reverence and admiration? He had that power.

But it wasn't fear that he generated, it was respect. He generated a natural respect by his very presence. His ki was so strong; he would hold a sword and ki would sweep around the room as he turned his hips and then dropped them. His technique was incredibly sharp.

YUUICHI NAKAGUCHI

O-Sensei's eyes were gentle; they were like crystals. They were magnificent. If he looked at you a certain way, you couldn't do anything.

MOTOMICHI ANNO

After WWII, O-Sensei's attitude toward others changed. His fierce gaze had become tender. One felt like getting close to him. O-Sensei said, "Until now all budo has been for destruction. It was for killing. If people behave this way again, it will result in another terrible time. Budo must give joy and happiness to the partner. It must be the budo of love.

You must give your partner joy. Therefore, you must become able to immediately see your partner's ki. You must train to be able to immediately understand your partner's ki at the moment of engagement. You must unify speech, body, and mind. You must become one with the workings of all things in the universe, with kami and the force of nature. Body, speech, and mind; these three must be in harmony with the working of the universe. If you do that, true budo will be born. The budo of destroying others will become the budo of giving happiness and consideration to others."

MICHIO HIKITSUCHI

Over the years I became more and more impressed with O-Sensei's goodness. There just wasn't anything bad or evil in O-Sensei at all. He was just tremendous goodness.

GUJI MUNETAKA KUKI

O-Sensei was always very kind.

MASAKI TANI

The most important thing O-Sensei taught was to be able to understand and accept each person, each one's individual character. Besides his budo, he was a man of extraordinary and noble character. He had a personal magnetism that went beyond his appeal as a martial artist.

YUUICHI NAKAGUCHI

O-Sensei himself said that the most important thing is love— Aikido has as its aim harmony among human beings.

NOBUYOSHI TAMURA

O-Sensei's technique was spiral in nature and all his moves were in a natural spiral fashion. O-Sensei always unified himself with the universe; he was able to control others from that stance. That's why, even though I was thrown hard, I was never afraid of the throw.

MOTOMICHI ANNO

O-Sensei felt that Aikido is about creation—with making more and more. He believed that every day should be fresh, new, and fuller than the last. He was always giving birth to new things.

SHINGENOBU OKUMURA

O-Sensei taught that it was important to speak gently and watch one's expression, because language can hurt or injure living people. Natural heart and natural words communicate without contrivance.

MOTOMICHI ANNO

The concept of *musubi*, which is important to Aikido, is the opposite of emptiness. *Musu* means "to give birth" and *hi* is "the spirit-fire of life." Thus musubi *(musu-hi)* implies the idea of the Holy Spirit continually giving birth. The productive and creative energy is musubi. In Shinto, the musubi concept is very, very important.

SHINGENOBU OKUMURA

O-Sensei gave me a scroll that says, "Do the Aikido that cannot be seen by the human eye." O-Sensei talked not just about harmony with your partners but also about harmony within yourself. He continually told students to keep forging, purifying, and polishing themselves.

ROBERT NADEAU

O-Sensei taught that love creates harmony, harmony creates happiness, happiness creates treasure. The spirit of creating world peace comes before waza. Without that spirit, your Aikido cannot progress. My most important direct lesson from O-Sensei was that with a sincere heart I must do everything as though it were life and death.

O-Sensei said to look at nature to understand the working of the kami. He told us to decide on the right path for us by observing the workings of the kami every day.

MICHIO HIKITSUCHI

O-Sensei embodied Aikido; there was something in him that was deeply inspiring. I was inspired by watching O-Sensei move. Many say that to be around him was inspiring. O-Sensei had a profound effect on his student's lives.

Aikido changed my life in more than one way. I knew a lot of really smart people when I was at Harvard as a graduate student. I knew a lot of brilliant, world famous professors, but I never respected them as human beings in any special way. They were brilliant, but either they had too many martinis for lunch, or they were male chauvinist pigs, or whatever. As human beings, they weren't special. They just had a very well-developed muscle in their head, and, just as weight lifters are not necessarily better human beings because they are weight lifters, the same was true for these thinkers.

But O-Sensei was different. He was the first human being that I had ever met that I felt this way about. Something was developing in him, and Aikido was a reflection of that. So, if you took all the Aikido waza away, it wouldn't matter; he'd still be this amazing person. Aikido was his art and he lived it.

ROBERT FRAGER

O-Sensei taught us that Aikido is a discipline of both the body and the mind. Skill is important, but it is no good without purity of heart. This thought is what led many people to follow O-Sensei. It wasn't just his excellent skills, because there were

*O-Sensei standing before Kumano Hongu Taisha. O-Sensei had
a deep faith in the kami of the Kumano area. He said that,
Agatsu Katsu hayahi no Mikoto is the name of a Kumano
kami. "Self Victory; always victorious" is the name of the diety.
So it means there is never any defeat.*

many with such skills. It was his goodwill that attracted many to him.

MAMORU SUGANUMA

O-Sensei said very clearly and emphatically that the truth of Aikido could be caught in a very short moment of time. "If you catch the secret," he said, "you can do what I do in three months." Now that there are people who have been training in Aikido for thirty, forty, and even fifty years, it has become apparent that it's not the length of time one studies that makes an O-Sensei. I myself have spent the last thirty years looking for that three-month secret.

ROBERT NADEAU

Once O-Sensei said, "I am on the Way and I think that I am being followed, but when I look back, I'm surprised that I can't see anybody." At the time, we deshi thought, "My God, we have trained ardently all this time! What *more* does he want?" At the time we couldn't understand; we were too young. But it was the student's obligation to understand what he was saying when he used language like this.

NOBUYOSHI TAMURA

My Kendo teacher used to say that *sen* has different levels: *sen sen no sen* (prior initiative), *tai no sen* (mutual initiative), and *go no sen* (late initiative). In the company of a fellow student who also had a Kendo background, we approached O-Sensei and asked him about this. We said that as we understood Aikido, it is go no sen, completely defensive.

O-Sensei blew up and said, "After all these years, you fellows haven't figured any of this out yet! Don't you realize that there's only one sen?" O-Sensei felt very strongly that, in Aikido, it's not right to divide sen up.

SHINGENOBU OKUMURA

O-Sensei was interested in making sincere human beings. O-Sensei was the most sincere, most pure person. But even though he had this purpose, he never forced others; he understood that different people think differently. He said that each of us must make ourselves sincere, that he can introduce us to the path but that each person must walk it for himself. O-Sensei said, "I can only explain to you what the kami have told me." He never ordered anyone.

He also told us to have a sense of gratitude. Be thankful to others and to nature. Without gratitude we cannot become true human beings. The power of nature, the sun, gives us everything. When rain falls, the field produces rice. Fruit and grain grow. This is the gift of the earth. Therefore the keiko is very important.

MICHIO HIKITSUCHI

Many students say O-Sensei was difficult to understand. I think they just lacked patience and knowledge. If you studied and thought about what he was saying, it was not so difficult to understand. I was motivated to do a column of O-Sensei's thought in the Aikido newspaper in order to preserve O-Sensei's teachings.

SADATERU ARIKAWA

For a time I was editor of an English-language publication from Aikikai Hombu Dojo called *Aikido*. When I first took the position of editor, it became clear to me that the publication angered O-Sensei. O-Sensei even told me that he didn't like it. I knew that O-Sensei didn't anger without cause, so I took it upon myself to discover why O-Sensei didn't like the publication. When I took a hard look at some of the issues, it became clear to me that what was missing in every issue was O-Sensei; there were no words or images of O-Sensei, the founder of Aikido. I made sure there were photos and words of O-Sensei in the forthcoming issues, and every time afterward that I took the paper to O-Sensei, O-Sensei would smile and say, "Thank you."

ROBERT NADEAU

O-Sensei was a man who was totally natural in his posture and movement. One student says that he learned that one's posture and heart should be natural from watching O-Sensei.

MOTOMICHI ANNO

When I lived in Iwama, O-Sensei was developing Aikido as an art for peaceful times. Before then, many people had come to study with him to learn skills for combat and conquest even though O-Sensei had realized that the spirit of martial arts is love. But for O-Sensei, the period in Iwama after WWII was a quiet time of reflection and rebuilding. O-Sensei's vision was deepened through his life of farming and his work with students. O-Sensei often talked about *ai* as love, but he didn't talk about war.

KAZUAKI TANAHASHI

O-Sensei's words and actions were always matched and neither ever showed any openings. There were no openings in either his technique or his spirit. He was mysterious.

MOTOMICHI ANNO

The Founder used to talk about the triangle, the circle, and the square quite often. He used to say that technique starts with a triangle and moves in a circular way to a pin. He described technique in philosophical terms.

MORIHIRO SAITO

When meeting O-Sensei, one had the feeling that he was not an ordinary person. There was something special about him. He had a marvelous appearance. The impression that remains with me is not so much O-Sensei's technique on the mat but how he appeared when he was sitting in a room.

O-Sensei would sit in a room used for changing clothes at the old dojo in Shingu where I practiced. When O-Sensei was visiting, students didn't use that room for changing clothes. One day I went early and passed the room. O-Sensei was sitting there by himself and said, "Boy, come here." He told me that I was a serious student and was honest and gentle *(sunao)*. That has remained with me my whole life. I thought that I might not be great at technique, but I could always be honest and gentle.

As a result, the most important lesson I learned from O-Sensei is the importance of sunao: it is best to be unaffected and uncontrived and to be natural. The form that emerges naturally from your heart and is one with nature and is not constructed is best.

MOTOMICHI ANNO

O-Sensei taught that it was really important for martial artists to never loose their awareness. To drive this point home, O-Sensei would often tell the story of an accomplished martial arts master who drank and, having become drunk, was attacked and killed.

MOTOICHI YANASE

O-Sensei often talked about the three shapes: triangle, circle, and square. He would often inscribe them in the air and brush them on paper. It was clear that these three shapes were extremely important, but it wasn't easy to understand why.

New students generally didn't ask O-Sensei questions; they just felt it wasn't appropriate. One day after spring cleaning at the Iwama farm, I got up the courage to ask O-Sensei what these shapes meant. So I said, "Sensei, would you tell me the significance of the triangle, circle, and square?" O-Sensei nodded, looked down at the ground, looked at me, looked up, looked back down at the ground, thought for a minute, and then said, "Find out yourself." Initially, I was incensed. I thought O-Sensei could have said something.

But a Japanese carpenter with whom I apprenticed taught me that the only way to make knowledge one's own is to steal it—what is given is quickly forgotten. So I came to see that what O-Sensei said to me was the kindest thing he could have said.

TERRY DOBSON

One day while in a taxicab with O-Sensei, I asked him a question, "Sensei, what is the right attitude toward your Aikido?" O-Sensei smiled and said, "Your attitude toward your partner should be like a parent to a child." Unconditionally loving, but also leading them and expecting they will follow.

ROBERT FRAGER

I once asked O-Sensei, "How can you see God?" O-Sensei pointed at himself and then at me, "My God perceives your God."

MITSUGI SAOTOME

I read in a book that the Founder said he wanted everybody to practice "enjoyably." So, one time I asked O-Sensei about this. O-Sensei said, "Yes, you must practice enjoyably. There is no sense practicing when everybody suffers. If there's good feeling, the ki comes out. So the dojo will be full of ki."

Then I asked him if he believed in tournaments (shiai). With his face cast down, O-Sensei said, "No, definitely not. The person who wins is happy, but there's always a loser. You cannot only have a winner. The person who loses is not happy. The loser is going to train hard so that he can beat the winner. If you have somebody trying to beat you, you have an enemy— a friendly enemy, but he is still trying to beat you. Why not try to beat the ultimate person? Yourself."

TAKASHI NONAKA

In 1924 O-Sensei accompanied Deguchi (Onisaburo Deguchi was one of the founders of Omotokyo.) to Manchuria, seeking a place to serve as the spiritual center for "a world cooperative of people of five races and colors," a vision of Omotokyo (a Shinto sect) based on the idea that all teachings evolved from a single origin. Their path led them into many tense encounters with armed bandits and professional soldiers. By this time, O-Sensei had reached such an advanced level of spiritual awareness that when fired upon, he would perceive the aggression in the form of a small point of light immediately preceding the bullet. O-Sensei described his experience: "Before the opponent could pull the trigger, his intention to kill would form into a ball of spiritual light and fly at me. If I evaded this ball of light, no bullet could touch me."

MITSUGI SAOTOME

When O-Sensei was in Manchuria, he was able to dodge bullets—he knew where they were going to go. So, O-Sensei's clairvoyant power was highly developed. O-Sensei was a person who had that special kind of power.

SHINGENOBU OKUMURA

I have many of O-Sensei's calligraphy works, because we would often practice Shodo together when O-Sensei would visit my dojo in Osaka. The calligraphy, which says *"masaka agatsu katsuhayahi,"* reminds me of a very important lesson that O-Sensei taught me. O-Sensei said that you must first win over the self or ego, and that if you can't do that, then there is no point in coming to class. Secondly, he said that one should seek for the correctness or the proper truth of one's life. Then if you can win over the self and find your proper and correct life's purpose, then the speed beyond light will manifest in your technique. The truth of victory must be found within the self. Once you win over the self, your technique has the speed of light.

SEISEKI ABE

The most basic thing to O-Sensei's Aikido was *takemusu* (spontaneous creation of protective or martial arts.) Not *takemusu aikido*, just takemusu. I learned it was important to study continuously and to ask deep questions. O-Sensei liked to talk about the breath of kami: O-Sensei called it "the *himizu* breath." The word *himizu* (cosmic) is written by drawing a cross. The vertical is fire; the horizontal is water. This relates to misogi, the practice of purification, and to the male/female pair, Izanagi and Izanami, and the creation of the universe. O-Sensei would talk about these things when he talked to me about takemusu. O-Sensei said that takemusu is the thing that enlivens Aikido.

I began to understand these things much later. O-Sensei's talk left a deep impression on me.

SADATERU ARIKAWA

O-Sensei said that if you look at the form of nature, you will understand Aikido. Harmony is most important. To become harmonious, you must work to make all edges round. In harmony there are no edges, only roundness. The seed is round, the plants have round stems. Most important is if there is harmony,

*Students striking at O-Sensei, who had just been standing
in the middle of this circle of five students. O-Sensei, just
having escaped from the middle of this circle of sword-bearing
students. In O-Sensei's demonstrations he would often seem
to defy physics by becoming immovable or, as depicted here,
by moving faster than an observer's eye.*

there is affection, love. Love is the benevolent heart. You must have respect for others. It is important to create this. If you have a benevolent heart, you can give love and from there arises harmony. When harmony is born, happiness is born. Thus, love gives birth to harmony and harmony gives birth to happiness. Happiness gives birth to treasure. We humans must take care of all of nature in place of the kami. The kami never taught people to kill each other. If we don't give happiness and joy, we lose the treasure; this treasure is spiritual. It is not gold or diamonds. O-Sensei said that it is most important to teach this lesson so that the world becomes one family. It is not a matter of strong waza. Aikido is for the purpose of teaching that, with the heart of love, we can make all one family. That is its purpose.

MICHIO HIKITSUCHI

O-Sensei taught me that through Aikido we learn how to interpret another person's mind so that we can cooperate and avoid fighting. He taught me that we can achieve something we really want, not by fighting but by being harmonious. That's why it is important to work together; we both benefit. We make sure that the other side is protected instead of pushing aside or hurting the other side. We have to think of the benefits of the other side. When we sort of corroborate with that, ki force moves in a good direction. When we struggle in an attempt to get out of something, then we actually block the flow of ki. O-Sensei would say Aikido is nonresistant and then he wouldn't resist, he just extended and down we'd go. No struggles, just winning.

O-Sensei was showing us something important when he did his demonstrations of Aikido. There was something distant in his demonstration; O-Sensei was doing a dance.

KAZUAKI TANAHASHI

O-Sensei always emphasized *wa* (harmony) in *aiki*. When I came back from Europe, I told O-Sensei that in order for me to win tournaments, I needed something more than aiki; I had to use different *Bujitsu*. O-Sensei scolded me, "Aiki is not a matter of winning and losing. I am disappointed that you have not realized that yet."

MINORU MOCHIZUKI

My father—Major Shigeo Tanahashi—was a staff officer in the Imperial Military Headquarters before WWII. He was also a student of O-Sensei's. He moved close to Hombu Dojo in 1934. I remember my father saying "O-Sensei really understood the ultimate secret of martial arts: the ultimate secret of martial arts is that you don't lose if you don't fight."

Unfortunately, O-Sensei's teaching could not flower in the Japan of the late 1930s, but the modern world is ready to take his teaching seriously. That spirit of love and harmony, and then being in touch with a higher source; these things are really important in addition to doing your practice.

KAZUAKI TANAHASHI

Even while O-Sensei was developing the art, he prayed that Aikido would spread around the world. He felt that previous martial arts, in which each blow was intended to cause death, were not good for the world. He felt that the world needed an Aikido of "divine techniques and no killing."

SHINGENOBU OKUMURA

The attraction of O-Sensei was that he was so positive; it was very encouraging to see a human being who cultivated such a positive power. It is wonderful that Aikido is not destructive, but life affirming, helping the world, loving all people. It is wonderful that Aikido is about being peaceful and expanding peace, spreading peace all over the world. Aikido is a widely practiced martial art. Part of the reason is that Aikido is a very positive cultivating power; not a controlling or defeating power, but the power to love and to be helpful and harmonious. This comes from O-Sensei's enlightenment.

Aikido is a combination of enormous strength and the training it takes to cultivate it further. Then there is almost no limit once you get to the point of O-Sensei. It is a long way to go and then there is always the way for us to cultivate more and more strength. Then cultivate the understanding of love and harmony. Maybe this is too commonplace to say. It is kind of ironical that love can be very strong.

KAZUAKI TANAHASHI

The most common topic of O-Sensei's conversation was about the path that humans needed to take to live in the world, about his views of life. He was very concerned about humanity and human life, and he didn't talk so much about the kami as a specific religion, but about more practical matters regarding human beings. People thought O-Sensei himself was a kind of living Buddha, and they would gather around him.

GUJI MUNETAKA KUKI

Every morning, he would make an offering at the dojo, pray to the four directions, and ask for prosperity for 10,000 years.

These rituals were important to him. O-Sensei's norito chanting was his personal practice. Most of the time he did not invite any of his students to join him.

O-Sensei would usually pray by himself, reciting the Misogi No Norito; then he would chant *"hito, futa, mi, yo, itsu, muyu, nana, ya, koko-no, tari, momo, chi, yorozu"* (It means "1, 2, 3, 4, 5, 6, 7, 8, 9, 10, 100, 1,000, 10,000"). O-Sensei would chant this over and over in a very high tone. O-Sensei's voice was amazing when he was chanting. It was full strength and very high. My mother just hated it.

O-Sensei didn't see Aikido as just a kind of martial art; he saw it as an art that brings peace to the world.

KAZUAKI TANAHASHI

O-Sensei used to say that the purpose of Aikido wasn't to defeat another person and the purpose of Aikido was not to attack others, but to be able to protect yourself, that the spirit of Aikido is always the spirit of protection not the spirit of conflict.

GUJI MUNETAKA KUKI

I am the son of a priest, but I didn't really think about doing the waterfall practice as my personal practice until I saw O-Sensei. When I saw O-Sensei under the waterfall, he looked divine, and he looked like a deity himself as he stood there under the water, saying the Norito. I was incredibly moved by that and motivated to do it myself. When I saw O-Sensei do the practice, I thought it must be a very significant practice. I used to watch my father go under the waterfall right by our house every day. I had that image in my head of my father doing that every day, but when I saw O-Sensei do that here, it suddenly just all came together for me. I realized I was the one who had to carry on the family tradition and it was important for me to do this practice. O-Sensei's influence on me is just very large.

GUJI YUKITAKA YAMAMOTO

I saw O-Sensei praying and noticed that often O-Sensei is holding the jo, or sword, straight up, vertically. This is a traditional Shinto way of relating to the deities; it is like putting up a spiritual antenna to connect with the deities high up in heaven. For example, he says that, in the Noh play, when you see people walking with a twig of bamboo held vertically, one is to understand that they represent people who are connected with another world.

So we can understand O-Sensei was someone whose mind was not only in the here and now but also was higher up in the vast universal space, perhaps able to draw energy from up there. Also, farming, walking outside in nature, and in a way, being content with nature, are ways of offering prayers to a higher realm. O-Sensei was very involved with nature. Often O-Sensei would pray while holding and moving a staff. Even when he was showing martial arts, he was showing prayers and this was happening all the time.

O-Sensei was always talking about different types of spirit and souls and how things work in the mythic world. As young boys, we often felt bored with the nightly routine of God stuff. This was a kind of a mask. We thought that to work with O-Sensei we had to put up with him about this. We viewed all this as some kind of archaic world and we didn't want it; we wanted the kind of technique O-Sensei was doing. But actually, the real secret of O-Sensei's power comes from all that he was doing, so to ignore this side of O-Sensei was a kind of great mistake.

113

At least I have a kind of respect—I have a deep respect—for that something that makes O-Sensei, O-Sensei. So, in a way I was not listening, but in another way I was in there and experiencing all this with him. That was maybe a great gate that he presented; that he was always presenting that high realm. Then, to sort of make me understand this kind of spiritual experience becomes the basic fundamental power for any kind of work, any kind of art, any kind of work or service for the world, but that is really essential.

KAZUAKI TANAHASHI

I feel very fortunate to have had O-Sensei as a teacher in my life. O-Sensei gave me a positive direction. O-Sensei was the salvation of my life.

O-Sensei was very strict, very serious. But he was also very humorous and positive. He was very positive in how he regarded society. O-Sensei spoke about political problems of all kinds, but he always expressed the hope for human happiness. This was his prayer.

MITSUGI SAOTOME

My father, Major Shigeo Tanahashi, was a war planner. In 1938 he became disturbed by the imminent plans for war with the United States. He went to his Aikido teacher with his concern. O-Sensei said, "I agree with you, Tanahashi-san. We must try as hard as possible to avoid the war. I would very much like you to work on it. You will have all my support."

In prewar Japan, however, any civilian or soldier who openly mentioned another nation's military supremacy or voiced the intention of preventing war would be arrested, tortured, and perhaps killed. So, Shigeo had to keep the involvement of O-Sensei in utmost secrecy to protect the master's life. Consultation with O-Sensei usually took place after Shigeo had joined the evening training at the Aikido Hombu Dojo.

The strategy to avoid the war obviously failed, and when O-Sensei heard about it, he saw Japan's inevitable path to war in the Pacific—and he also foresaw defeat. Tears in his eyes, O-Sensei held Shigeo's hands and said, "Tanahashi-san, our peace work is crushed now. Many, many people will suffer incredibly in the coming war. As a soldier you will have to fight. Always remember to take care of yourself. Let's trust that there will be another opportunity for us to work for peace."

At Shimbashi Station in Tokyo, O-Sensei, the founder of Aikido, was wearing his hakama and black kimono and carrying a cane. He had accompanied Tanahashi's family to see him off on a military transfer to Europe.

KAZUAKI TANAHASHI

Aikido is based on a philosophy that recognizes that, in the second half of the twentieth century, with the arrival of nuclear weapons and other forms of destructive power, the human race cannot go on in its old ways. O-Sensei thought that if we continue in the traditions of the past, one day all of humanity could be suddenly destroyed. We are at a point where we must say, "Stop!"

SHINGENOBU OKUMURA

One thing O-Sensei said was that when the war ended, the era of fighting was finished and he needed to give birth to takemusu aiki. He spent hours and hours in front of the shrine praying and thinking how to shape Aikido for the postwar era. His mind was like a computer generating new technique after new technique.

MORIHIRO SAITO

O-Sensei saw that, if humanity continued its murderous behavior, we wouldn't last much longer. He felt that we must put behind us the idea that killing is a solution.

SHINGENOBU OKUMURA

O-Sensei taught that Aikido creates an honest and pure person, someone of sincerity, someone who does not lie, someone who is undeceiving. In other words, Aikido creates a true human being.

O-Sensei thought that at the time of birth a baby doesn't think any thoughts. It is one with the kami. As the baby grows up, it is taught many things and in that process impurities are born. So it is without thought, being one with the kami, that we can return to our kami mind, a mind of love. We call this practice returning to kami mind/heart *chinkon*.

By pacifying our own spirit and returning to kami mind, we can receive the power of the kami. O-Sensei thought that the purpose of the teachings of Aikido is for returning to the kami and receiving the power of the kami.

Based on this understanding of the purpose of Aikido, its aim is for the peace of the world. The root and the foundation of Aikido is this. Talking about good or bad, new or old techniques is useless. Technique is just technique. We cannot understand Aikido without studying the essential spirit of Aikido. The object of this study is to create a person who is sincere and kind, who has a true heart. Physical technique exists as Aikido

O-Sensei was someone whose mind was not only in the here and now but also higher up in the vast universal space, drawing energy down from above. Often O-Sensei would pray while holding and moving a staff.

discipline. Putting aside the spirit and only doing physical technique, no matter how many times it is practiced, will not lead to understanding the heart of Aikido and will not lead to true technique. Just practicing technique will lead nowhere.

MICHIO HIKITSUCHI

O-Sensei said that the appropriateness of developing one's own techniques differs from person to person. Some need more time, and others less. People should follow their own rhythms.

NOBUYOSHI TAMURA

As O-Sensei got older and he knew his time was running out, he would talk about what was important to him, but people would often run away. He wanted everybody to get it, but just telling them wasn't going to do much good. He was talking about the source—the ultimate thing, "God."

HENRY KONO

O-Sensei's words are most important. Aikido cannot become a sport. If it is a sport, there will be mistakes and carelessness. That is not truth. If you want to be true, you must train with all your heart, all your strength. It should be like *shinkenshobu*, a contest with a live blade—as though you would lose your life with one error. Even if you are an upright person, you could become bad with one mistake. We must be careful not to make the smallest mistake. O-Sensei was the very model of a true human being.

MICHIO HIKITSUCHI

The atmosphere of an old-time Japanese person and modern Japanese person is very different. To an old-time Japanese mind, our connection to nature was very clear. I remember that when I talked to O-Sensei, I felt I was talking to a person of old times. This atmosphere that he had about him began to affect my attitude and thinking. I tried to pass O-Sensei's manner of speech on in the columns I prepared.

SADATERU ARIKAWA

O-Sensei from his deathbed sent for me. When I got there, O-Sensei simply said, *Onegaishimasu* (If you would be so kind). I was beside myself trying to figure out what it was O-Sensei was asking me to do. I would've done anything for my teacher. But O-Sensei didn't elaborate.

I spent the rest of my life talking about nonviolence and Aikido. I remembered O-Sensei talking about your responsibilities to your community, to other people. He also often said that it was very important to go back and talk about nonviolence. So I believed that O-Sensei's request was for me to return to the United States and talk about nonviolence.

TERRY DOBSON

When O-Sensei did certain exercises, he invoked the God of purification, but he himself said to his students that they didn't have to do the same. His view was that his students should be thinking about whatever God or Gods are sacred to *them*.

SHINGENOBU OKUMURA

During the final two weeks of his life, as I took my turn sitting at O-Sensei's bedside, I watched the familiar face beneath the wispy, white beard grow thinner day by day. I experienced a grief greater than any I had ever known as the many memories of O-Sensei's almost superhuman strength flooded his heart. Although O-Sensei's body was wasting away, his mind was sharp and his eyes had the clarity and peace of a child's. O-Sensei talked very little at this time, but communication was strong and he was always thinking of Aikido.

Two days before his death O-Sensei raised his frail body to a sitting position, looked at the students who were gathered there, and said, "You must not worry about this old man. All physical life is limited. Within the course of nature, the physical being must change, but the spirit will never die. Soon I will enter the spiritual world, but still I want to protect this world. That is now your task." He went into a deep meditation and after some time continued, "All my students must remember, I did not create Aikido. Aiki is the wisdom of God; Aikido is the Way of the laws that He created."

MITSUGI SAOTOME

Glossary

AI   One Japanese word pronounced *ai* means "union" or perhaps "harmony"; another means "love." (It is the first that
appears in the name "Aikido," but the founder of the art
may have intended a pun.)

AIKI   Literally, "confluence of life-energy." To perform a technique with aiki is to blend physically and mentally with
one's attacker.

AIKIDO   Literally, "the Way of confluent energy"; sometimes
more loosely translated as "the Art of Peace." A modern
Japanese martial art, which—though useful in self-
defense— emphasizes harmony, cooperation, and nonre-

sistance. Aikido's founder, Morihei Ueshiba, realized that the essence of budo (martial Way) is love, and he urged his students and followers to act in "the spirit of loving protection for all of God's creation."

BLACKBELT   One who has passed beyond the *kyu* (beginning) levels of training of a Japanese martial art to the *dan* (more advanced) levels. In Aikido, as in other Japanese martial arts, lower ranked students wear white or colored belts (*obi*), while more advanced students wear black belts.

BO   A long wooden staff sometimes used in Aikido practice.

BOKKEN   A wooden sword approximating the size and shape of a samurai sword.

BU   Japanese term meaning "martial" or "military."

BUDO   Literally "a martial path" or "martial Way." At the beginning of the twentieth century, when it became clear that traditional samurai battlefield techniques would not be of much use in subsequent warfare, Japanese Bujitsu (systems of fighting techniques) were transformed into budo, or modern Japanese martial arts. In some cases, they were transformed into sports. For example, Kenjitsu (battlefield sword techniques) became the sport of Kendo, and Jujitsu became the sport of Judo. In other cases, the result of the transformation was a *Do* (an art of spiritual development).

BUDOKA   A student of martial or warrior Ways.

BUJITSU   *See* Budo.

BUSHIDO   Literally, "the Way of the warrior or samurai." The code of the warrior class of feudal Japan.

CHINKON   Literally, "calming down." A meditation technique.

DESHI   A student or, more precisely, an apprentice or disciple.

DOGI   The practice uniform worn in most Japanese martial arts, also called a "keikogi," or a "gi" for short.

DOJO   Literally, "place of the Way." A training hall or school of
    Japanese martial arts.

DOSHU   The leader of the Way; hereditary head of world
    Aikido. The second Doshu of Aikido was the founder's
    son (Kisshomaru Ueshiba Sensei), and the third is the
    founder's grandson (Moriteru Ueshiba Sensei).

GASSHUKU   A special extended training period during which
    students eat, sleep, and train together.

GETA   Japanese shoes or sandals.

GO NO SEN   A technical term in Kendo and other Japanese
    martial arts sometimes translated as "late initiative."

GUJI   The chief priest of a Shinto shrine.

HAKAMA   Baggy, skirt-like pants often worn as part of the tra-
    ditional Aikido uniform.

HANMI   An Aikido stance.

HAORI   A Japanese half-coat.

HIMIZU   A symbol in which fire and water are represented by
    a vertical line crossing a horizontal line. Put inside a cir-
    cle, it depicts a person's place in the universe.

IAIDO   The Way of drawing the sword.

IKKYO   Literally, "first lesson." One of Aikido's basic tech-
    niques.

IKKYO SUWARIWAZA   Ikkyo performed from a seated position.

IRIMINAGE   One of Aikido's basic throws.

JI   An old man.

JO   A wooden staff used in Aikido training.

JUDO   A Japanese martial art developed, like Aikido, from Ju-
    jitsu's unarmed fighting techniques. Unlike Aikido, Judo
    is often practiced as a competitive sport.

JUJITSU   A Japanese martial art that uses leverage and weight
    placement to neutralize attacks.

KAMI   A divine energy or being.

KAMIDANA   A household altar. Kamidana sometimes appear on the main walls of Aikido dojos.

KARATE   Literally, "empty hand" or perhaps originally "Chinese hand." An Okinawan striking and kicking art out of which Japanese Karate-do arose.

KEIKO   Practice or training, especially training in traditional Japanese martial arts forms.

KEIKOGI   A training uniform.

KENDO   Literally, "the Way of the sword or blade." A Japanese martial art, sometimes practiced as a sport, in which *shinai* (split bamboo sticks) are used to simulate samurai swords.

KI   Universal energy or life force.

KIAI   A spirited shout or yell.

KIHON   A Japanese term for "basic," used in the phrase *kihon waza*, which means "basic technique."

KIMONO   Part of a Japanese dressing gown or costume made up of a loose outer garment with a sash.

KOBUDO   Traditional or ancient budo.

KOJIKI   One of the sacred books of Shinto, Japan's indigenous religion, the *Kojiki* contains an account of the creation of the world.

KOKYU   Literally, "inhale/exhale." The cycle of breath. Some of Aikido's throwing techniques are called *kokyu nage* (breath throws) because of their timing and feel.

KOKYU WAZA   Literally, "breath techniques." *See* kokyu.

KOTEGAESHI   One of Aikido's basic wrist-locking techniques.

KOTODAMA   Literally, "word spirit." A spiritual practice centered around words or voiced sounds.

MANJU   A bun with a bean-jam filling.

MISOGI   Purification practice.

MUSUBI   Connection. *Ki-musubi* is "connection of energies."

NIDAN   A second-level blackbelt.

NOH A form of traditional Japanese musical theater.

NORITO A Shinto prayer.

OFURO A Japanese bath.

OHARAI NORITO A purification prayer.

OKUSAMA Lady of the house or a married lady.

OKASHI A Japanese snack food.

OMOTOKYO A Shinto-based religion founded toward the end of the nineteenth century. While Aikido's founder may not have formally been a member of the Omotokyo, he was certainly inspired by Omotokyo's leader, Onisaburo Deguchi.

REI A bow or salute. More generally, courtesy or etiquette.

REIGI Strict etiquette or formality.

SAMURAI A member of the warrior class of feudal Japan.

SANDAN A third-level blackbelt.

SEIZA A Japanese sitting position, with shins on the floor.

SEN Initiative.

SEN SEN NO SEN A technical term used in Kendo and other Japanese martial arts that is sometimes translated as "prior initiative."

SENDAI A predecessor or someone of the previous generation.

SENSEI Literally, "one born before." A term of respect for a teacher or elder.

SHIATSU A system of therapy often involving massage or finger pressure.

SHIHONAGE Literally, "four direction throw." One of Aikido's basic techniques.

SHIN Mind, heart, or spirit.

SHINAI A split-bamboo practice sword.

SHINKENSHOBU Severe training; practicing as if one's life depended on it.

SHINTO Japanese folk religion, closely aligned with nature.

SHODAN   A first-level blackbelt.

SHODO   Literally, "the Way of the brush." The art of Japanese calligraphy.

SHOMENUCHI   An overhead strike often used in Aikido practice.

SHUGYO   Severe training.

SUMO   A Japanese form of wrestling.

SUNAO   Gentle and honest.

SUKI   An unguarded opening.

SUWARIWAZA   Aikido technique in which both the attacker and defender are seated.

TAI NO SEN   A technical term in Kendo and other Japanese martial arts sometimes translated as "mutual initiative."

TAKEMUSU   Spontaneous creation of protective or martial arts.

TAMAGUSHI   An offering.

TATAMI   Traditional straw mats, sometimes used in dojos.

UCHI DESHI   A live-in student or disciple.

UDON   A type of Japanese noodle.

UKE   In paired Aikido practice, the partner who attacks and receives the technique.

UKEMI   Arts of the uke, which include methods of attacking and falling.

WA   Peace.

WAZA   Technique.

YANG   In Chinese philosophy, the active universal principle.

YIN   In Chinese philosophy, the passive universal principle.

YONKYO   Literally, "fourth lesson." In yonkyo, an attacker is controlled by the arm, sometimes with a nerve pinch.

ZEN   A Japanese offshoot of Buddhism emphasizing meditation and directed toward enlightenment.

Contributors

Seiseki Abe, Aikido 10th dan, is the chief instructor of Amano Takemusu Aiki Juku dojo in Osaka, Japan. He is also a master calligrapher and had a close relationship with O-Sensei in brushwork, as well as in the role of an Aikido student.

Kenshiro Abbe, Judo 8th dan, a Judo champion and teacher. He was the chief instructor of the Kyoto police and Doshisha University. He was the first to teach Aikido in the United Kingdom

Motomichi Anno studied Aikido at Aikido Kumano Juku Dojo with O-Sensei and Hikitsuchi Sensei after WWII. He was one of the senior teachers there. He founded his own school in Kumano City more than thirty years ago.

Sadateru Arikawa began Aikido with O-Sensei in 1947. He served for fifteen years as editor of Aikido's first Japanese newsletter. He continues to teach as a senior instructor at Aikikai Hombu Dojo.

Ken Cottier is a direct student of O-Sensei's who has practiced since the early 1960s. Cottier Sensei is the senior instructor and president of the Hong Kong Aikido Association.

Terry Dobson was an American who lived among O-Sensei's uchi deshi at Aikikai Hombu Dojo in Tokyo in the 1960s. He returned to the United States in the early 1970s and was a pioneer in spreading Aikido in America. He passed away in 1992.

Robert Frager is an American who studied with O-Sensei at Aikikai Hombu Dojo in the early 1960s. When he returned to America, he founded the Institute of Transpersonal Psychology in Mountain View, California, where he teaches Aikido.

Mary Heiny is an American who began studying Aikido at Aikikai Hombu Dojo after observing O-Sensei in class. She also trained in Shingu, Japan, under Michio Hikitsuchi. Currently she resides in Seattle, Washington, and teaches Aikido around the world.

Michio Hikitsuchi, Aikido 10th dan, is chief instructor of the Aikido Kumano Juku Dojo in Shingu, Japan, and longtime student of O-Sensei's.

Ayako Ishiwata is the head of Iwata Shokai Company, Ltd., in Tokyo, Japan, a company that makes keikogi and hakama for purchase at Aikikai Hombu Dojo.

Henry Kono is a Canadian Aikido instructor who studied with O-Sensei at Aikikai Hombu Dojo after WWII in the early 1960s. He currently lives in Canada and teaches Aikido around the world.

Guji Munetaka Kuki is the head priest at Kumano Hongu Taisha in the Kumano mountains on the Wakayama Peninsula, Japan. He first met O-Sensei when he was a young boy, when his father was Guji and O-Sensei visited the shrine.

Ietaka Kuki is Guji Kuki's son.

Virginia Mayhew is an American who studied at Aikikai Hombu Dojo. She founded the New York Aikikai and the Hong Kong Aikikai, both of which are still operating today.

Minoru Mochizuki is the founder of Yoseikan, an amalgam of Judo, Aikido, and Karate. Originally a Judo student, he was sent by the founder of Judo, Jigoro Kano, to study with O-Sensei in 1930.

Robert Nadeau is an American Aikido instructor who studied at Aikikai Hombu Dojo in the early 1960s. Nadeau Sensei teaches Aikido in San Jose, California, and around the world.

Yuuichi Nakaguchi studied Aikido at Aikido Kumano Juku Dojo in Shingu, Japan, with O-Sensei and Hikitsuchi Sensei after WWII. He continues to practice and teach there.

Shoji Nishio practiced at the Aikikai Hombu Dojo. He is an advanced practitioner of Judo, Karate, and *Iaido* (the art of drawing the sword) as well.

Takashi Nonaka started studying Aikido in Hawaii after seeing an Aikido demonstration by Koichi Tohei in 1955. Nonaka visited O-Sensei in 1968 while he was visiting Japan. Nonaka

Sensei teaches Aikido in Hawaii and has served as president of the Hawaii Ki Society.

Shingenobu Okumura began his Aikido training under Kenji Tomiki in Manchuria in 1938. He became part of the teaching staff at Aikikai Hombu Dojo in the early 1950s and trained under O-Sensei. He currently teaches at Hombu Dojo.

Morihiro Saito was a student of O-Sensei's and lived with him in the Iwama countryside after WWII. He was head of Ibaragi dojo and guardian of the Aiki shrine in Iwama, Japan. He passed away in May, 2002.

Mitsugi Saotome was an uchi deshi of O-Sensei's from 1960 and taught at Aikikai Hombu Dojo until O-Sensei's death in 1969. He then moved to the United States and was a creative force in developing Aikido there. He is currently head of Aikido Schools of Ueshiba.

Mamoru Suganuma entered the Aikikai Hombu Dojo as an uchi deshi in 1964. He is chief instructor of the Aikido Shohei Juku in Fukuoka-shi, Japan.

Shin'ichi Suzuki was a student of Koichi Tohei, founder of Shinshin Toitsu Aikido. He visited Aikikai Hombu Dojo while O-Sensei was still teaching, and Koichi Tohei was still a senior instructor there. He is head of Maui Aikido Ki Society in Maui, Hawaii.

Nobuyoshi Tamura entered Aikikai Hombu Dojo in 1953 as an uchi deshi. He left in 1964 to develop Aikido in France. He is currently head of the Federation Francaise d'Aikido et de Budo.

Kazuaki Tanahashi is an author, artist, and environmentalist, who as a young man lived in the Iwama countryside with

O-Sensei and trained with him. He helped to translate *Aikido*, a book by Kisshomaru Ueshiba, the late Doshu, into English.

Masaki Tani was a student at Aikikai Hombu Dojo during O-Sensei's lifetime. He presently works in the International Department of Hombu Dojo and continues to train.

Moriteru Ueshiba is the grandson of Morihei Ueshiba O-Sensei. He is the current Doshu (hereditary head of world Aikido) and presides over Aikido World Headquarters in Tokyo, Japan. He continues to teach worldwide, as well as maintaining a teaching schedule at Aikikai Hombu Dojo.

Yoshimitsu Yamada entered Aikikai Hombu dojo as uchi deshi in 1956. He left in 1964 to take over the New York Aikikai in New York City. He has been instrumental in the development of Aikido in America through his large organization, the United States Aikido Federation.

Guji Yukitaka Yamamoto is the ninety-sixth chief priest of the Tsubaki Grand Shrine in Mie Prefecture in Japan. As a boy, he knew O-Sensei when O-Sensei came to Tsubaki shrine and visited with Yukitaka Yamamoto's father, who was the Guji before him.

Motoichi Yanase studied Aikido at Aikido Kumano Juku Dojo in Shingu, Japan, with O-Sensei and Hikitsuchi Sensei after WWII. He was one of the senior teachers there. He continues to live in Shingu and practice Aikido.

Credits

All of the stories in this book except for those mentioned below are reprinted with permission from *Aikido Today Magazine*, Claremont, California. *www.aiki.com*

Kenshiro Abbe's story on page 11 is a story to be published in a forthcoming book, *Positive Aikido, Forty-five Years of Traditional Teaching and Training*, by Dave Rogers. It is included here with permission given.

Terry Dobson's stories on pages 16, 80, 81, and 93 are reprinted from *It's A Lot Like Dancing: An Aikido Journey* by

Contact Information

Susan Perry can be reached at *Aikido Today Magazine*, P.O. Box 1060, Claremont, CA 91711-1060. Telephone: (909) 624-7770. Fax: (909) 398-1840. Email: *atm@aiki.com*